Maintaining the Competitive Advantage in Artificial Intelligence and Machine Learning

RAND WALTZMAN, LILLIAN ABLON, CHRISTIAN CURRIDEN, GAVIN S. HARTNETT, MAYNARD A. HOLLIDAY, LOGAN MA, BRIAN NICHIPORUK, ANDREW SCOBELL, DANIELLE C. TARRAF

Prepared for the United States Air Force
Approved for public release; distribution unlimited

 PROJECT AIR FORCE

For more information on this publication, visit www.rand.org/t/RRA200-1

Library of Congress Cataloging-in-Publication Data is available for this publication.
ISBN: 978-1-9774-0525-8

Published by the RAND Corporation, Santa Monica, Calif.
© Copyright 2020 RAND Corporation
RAND® is a registered trademark.

Support RAND
Make a tax-deductible charitable contribution at
www.rand.org/giving/contribute

www.rand.org

Preface

Artificial intelligence (AI) technologies hold the potential for becoming critical force multipliers in future military capabilities. Indeed, China has identified AI as key to enhancing national competitiveness and protecting national security and has put forth a national AI plan representing a whole-of-society approach that is backed by significant investments. The plan is guided by a set of milestone goals intended to position the People's Republic of China as the world's leader in AI innovation by 2030.

In spring 2018, given the potential significance of AI technologies for the U.S. Department of Defense (DoD) and national security, the Vice Chief of the Air Force asked RAND to examine the competitive standing of the United States relative to China. If DoD has a competitive advantage, what should it do to maintain it? If DoD does not have a competitive advantage, what should it do to achieve and maintain it? The results of this research will help inform the choices of the U.S. government in general and DoD in particular regarding ways— activities, posture, and capability development—that AI and machine learning technologies can be advanced and countered to meet present and future security challenges.

No expertise in AI is required to read and benefit from this report.

The research reported here was sponsored by the Vice Chief of Staff of the Air Force and conducted within the Force Modernization and Employment Program of RAND Project AIR FORCE as part of a fiscal year 2018 project, Maintaining the Competitive Edge in Artificial Intelligence and Machine Learning.

RAND Project AIR FORCE

RAND Project AIR FORCE (PAF), a division of the RAND Corporation, is the U.S. Air Force's federally funded research and development center for studies and analyses. PAF provides the Air Force with independent analyses of policy alternatives affecting the development, employment, combat readiness, and support of current and future air, space, and cyber forces. Research is conducted in four programs: Strategy and Doctrine; Force Modernization and Employment; Manpower, Personnel, and Training; and Resource Management. The research reported here was prepared under contract FA7014-16-D-1000.

Additional information about PAF is available on our website:
http://www.rand.org/paf/

This report documents work originally shared with the U.S. Air Force on January 28, 2019. The draft report, issued on December 31, 2018, was reviewed by formal peer reviewers and U.S. Air Force subject-matter experts.

Contents

Figures and Tables

Figures

Tables

Summary

Artificial intelligence (AI) technologies hold the potential to become critical force multipliers in future armed conflicts. Indeed, the People's Republic of China (PRC) has identified AI as key to "enhance national competitiveness and protect national security,"[1] and has put forth a national AI plan representing a whole-of-society approach that is backed by significant investments. The plan is guided by a set of milestone goals and is intended to position the PRC as the world's primary center of AI innovation by 2030. If the plan is successful, China will achieve a substantial military advantage over the United States and its allies, with significant negative strategic implications for the United States. With the 2017 *National Security Strategy* and 2018 *National Defense Strategy* identifying China as a great power competitor and given Beijing's focus on AI technology, how much of a lead does the United States have, and what do the United States and the U.S. Air Force (USAF) need to do to maintain that lead?[2]

For the purposes of this research, *AI* has been interpreted as the use of machine learning (ML) technologies to address a variety of application domains and problems, resulting in a multitude of capabilities, such as computer vision, natural-language processing, decision support, and command and control. ML is the field of computer science concerned with creating programs that "learn" from data using a large and evolving set of techniques grounded in statistics and mathematical optimization.

Against this backdrop, we identified the aspects of AI and ML that need whole-of-government attention to accelerate U.S. investment and implementation, as well as the investments and subsequent policies that would support U.S. commercial-academic-government AI and ML growth and protection. Our starting point was an assessment of current Chinese and U.S. AI and ML strategies; investment levels; and structural, systemic, and implementation differences that affect the development and adoption of AI in both nations.

Transforming AI advances into military capabilities requires leveraging advances in fundamental research or commercial industry, transitioning them to the military, assessing their effectiveness and suitability, and updating existing operational concepts or developing new ones to take advantage of the new capabilities. We thus assessed the potential for U.S.-China competition in AI and ML along five main dimensions: breakthrough fundamental research; advances in civilian industry (private sector, state owned, or state funded); development and

---

[1] State Council of the People's Republic of China, *A New Generation Artificial Intelligence Development Plan,* trans. Graham Webster, Rogier Creemers, Paul Triolo, and Elsa Kania, July 20, 2017.

[2] The White House, *National Security Strategy of the United States of America*, Washington, D.C., December 2017; James Mattis, *Summary of the 2018 National Defense Strategy of the United States of America: Sharpening the American Military's Competitive Edge*, Washington, D.C.: U.S. Department of Defense, 2018.

engineering to transition AI to the military; advances in validation, verification, testing, and evaluation (VVT&E); and operational concept development.

Our assessment is that, as of early 2020, the United States has a modest lead over the PRC in AI technology development. This is largely because the United States has had a substantial advantage over China in the advanced semiconductor design and manufacturing sector; the U.S. semiconductor industry is currently more capable and more advanced than that of the Chinese. A strong semiconductor industry is an essential foundation for good, solid AI research. China is attempting to erode this edge through massive government investment in the Chinese semiconductor industry.[3] Also, the Chinese semiconductor industry has the additional advantage of proximity to the enormous Chinese market.[4] This situation is further aggravated by the concurrent lack of a substantial U.S. industrial policy.[5] That being said, semiconductor design and fabrication are uniquely difficult processes. At present, Chinese firms continue to depend on American designs and lag behind South Korean and Taiwanese manufacturing.[6] Chinese attempts to find a shortcut to superiority by investing in newer types of chips and computing (as opposed to trying to unseat reigning American and allied companies in central processing unit production) may produce some fruit, but American and European companies are also highly active in exploring new computing technologies.[7] China has an advantage over the United States in the area of big data sets that are essential to the development of ML applications. This is in part because the Chinese regime and the large Chinese tech companies (such as Alibaba) are able to harvest much more personal data from the Chinese populace than U.S. tech firms can gather from the American populace because of the lack of real privacy laws and protections in China. Moreover, China has demonstrated both the capability and will to hack overseas databases so that it can leverage additional quantities of data. Also, the Chinese population is about four times

---

[3] For example,

> In the period since September 2014, numerous provinces and municipalities have established their own IC [integrated circuit] Funds, or received capital from the National IC Fund to establish other IC-related funds. Reports on the establishment of IC Funds in Hubei, Fujian, and Anhui provinces indicate the high degree of Chinese government involvement in establishing the funds in order to meet national strategic objectives. According to the SIA [Semiconductor Industry Association], provincial and municipal IC funds have raised a staggering sum—more than $80 billion. (Office of the U.S. Trade Representative, *Findings of the Investigation into China's Acts, Policies, and Practices Related to Technology Transfer, Intellectual Property, and Innovation Under Section 301 of the Trade Act of 1974*, Washington, D.C.: Executive Office of the President, March 22, 2018, pp. 93–94)

[4] Tekla S. Perry, "U.S. Semiconductor Industry Veterans Keep Wary Eyes on China," *IEEE Spectrum*, October 10, 2019.

[5] Perry, 2019.

[6] Jeffrey Ding, *Deciphering China's AI Dream: The Context, Components, Capabilities, and Consequences of China's Strategy to Lead the World in AI*, Oxford, U.K.: Future of Humanity Institute, University of Oxford, March 2018, pp. 17–19.

[7] "The Chips Are Down: The Semiconductor Industry and the Power of Globalisation," *The Economist,* December 1, 2018.

larger than the U.S. population, so Chinese tech firms have an inherently larger latent database to draw from, even without taking into account the lax privacy protections in China. In terms of which country has the advantage in venture capital financing or government funding, it is difficult to say. Overall, however, we believe that the Chinese advantage in data volume is not enough to overcome the U.S. edge in semiconductors. From our research, we judge that the United States currently appears to have a modest lead over the PRC in AI. But this lead leaves no room for complacency.

It is important for U.S. Department of Defense (DoD) leadership to keep in mind that, ultimately, the long-term prospects for DoD to maintain a lead over the Chinese military in AI-enabled systems, weapons, and operational concepts will, at least indirectly, depend on the ability of the United States to keep its edge over China in AI at the national level. Thus, USAF as an institution should do as much as it reasonably can to contribute to the overall national-level American effort to maintain the country's position as the world leader in AI. For example, a promising option is for the USAF to financially support promising dual-use AI research projects in the private sector through the judicious awarding of Air Force contracts. Another option would be for the Air Force to work with Defense Advanced Research Projects Agency to jointly sponsor and fund promising academic AI research that would have broad spinoff effects in the commercial sector. However, to maintain competitive advantage, the Air Force should devote the majority of its AI resources to the dimensions over which it has direct control: development and engineering to transition AI to the military, advances in VVT&E, and operational concept development.

It is difficult, if not impossible, to arrive at a definitive statement about which country has the lead in AI and what the trend lines look like using open-source materials alone. Indeed, there may not be a single lead. It was more useful to break AI into constitutive aspects and talk about various parts of the AI ecosystem. Some of the data we needed are not publicly available, and others—such as assessments of culture and institutional focus—do not lend themselves to quantitative assessment. Therefore, pursuing an overall metric to determine who was ahead in the AI ecosystem would have been challenging and of questionable merit. Overall, our data collection and analysis lead us to tentatively conclude that the United States has a narrow lead in a number of key areas of AI, although China has several advantages and a high degree of leadership focus on this issue. This assessment implies that the United States has little room for error and needs to focus its attention and resources on ensuring that China does not open up a substantial lead. AI appears likely to be a critical technology not only for the commercial economy that undergirds U.S. national power, including military applications and, most particularly, the aerospace domain.

We determined that breakthrough fundamental research is not a critical dimension for comparing U.S.-China relative competitive standing from a DoD perspective. Fundamental research, regardless of whether it is U.S., Chinese, or a U.S.-Chinese collaboration, is available to all. The results are presented at openly accessible international conferences and published in openly accessible international journals. Commercial industry is also not a critical dimension for competitive comparison. Nevertheless, whereas Chinese and American corporations had, until quite recently, been entangled with each other via business and research partnerships, China and the United States are in the process of economic and technological decoupling as a result of government decisions and policies in Beijing and Washington.

Industries with corporate headquarters in the United States and in China have a global outlook today. They seek to provide products and services wherever the market is, whether that is in the United States or China or anywhere else in the world. That said, government policies guide, restrict, and interfere with corporate decisions in each country. U.S. and Chinese corporations both pursue profit, but those in China, in particular, are subject to government guidance and interference.

In summary, we found that the critical dimensions for competitive comparison for DoD are promoting the development and engineering for transitioning AI to the military, making advances in VVT&E, and developing operational concepts for AI. Significantly, each of these dimensions is under direct DoD control.

To maintain a competitive edge, we recommend that DoD

- Manage expectations by developing and maintaining a forward-looking AI roadmap, highlighting realistic goals for DoD AI employment for the near (one to two years), middle (three to five years), and far (six to ten years) terms.
- Create an engineering pipeline under DoD control.
- Create and tailor VVT&E techniques for AI technologies.
- Create development, test, and evaluation processes for new operational concepts that employ AI.

Acknowledgments

The authors would like to thank James Chow, Program Director, and Elizabeth Bodine-Baron, Associate Program Director of the Force Modernization and Employment Program, RAND Project AIR FORCE, for their guidance and support. Special thanks go to our sponsors, Gen Stephen Wilson, Vice Chief of Staff of the Air Force, and Kenneth Bray, Acting Associate Deputy Chief of Staff for Intelligence, Surveillance, and Reconnaissance, Headquarters U.S. Air Force. We greatly appreciate Mr. Bray's support and enthusiasm for the project and have benefited greatly from his thoughtful guidance and feedback and our many discussions. The authors also wish to thank Scott Harold, Drew Lohn, and Osonde Osoba for their trenchant reviews.

Abbreviations

AI   artificial intelligence

CCP   Chinese Communist Party

DARPA   Defense Advanced Research Projects Agency

DoD   U.S. Department of Defense

IC   integrated circuit

ISR   intelligence, surveillance, and reconnaissance

MDO   multidomain operation

ML   machine learning

PLA   People's Liberation Army

PRC   People's Republic of China

R&D   research and development

ROTC   Reserve Officer Training Corps

S&T   science and technology

USAF   U.S. Air Force

VVT&E   verification, validation, test, and evaluation

1. Introduction

Artificial intelligence (AI) technologies hold the potential to become critical force multipliers in future armed conflicts. Indeed, the People's Republic of China (PRC) has identified AI as key to enhancing "national competitiveness and protect national security"[1] and has put forth a national AI plan representing a whole-of-society approach. China has backed that plan with significant investments and guides it through a set of milestone goals. The objective is to position the PRC as the world's primary center of AI innovation by 2030. Needless to say, if its national AI plan is successful, China will achieve a substantial military advantage over the United States and its allies, an advantage that will have significant negative strategic implications for the United States. The 2017 *National Security Strategy* and 2018 *National Defense Strategy* identified China as a great-power competitor.[2] Given Beijing's focus on AI technology, how much of a lead does the United States have, and what do the United States and the U.S. Air Force (USAF) need to do to maintain that lead?

Our objective here is to help inform the choices the U.S. government, particularly the U.S. Department of Defense (DoD) and USAF, make about activities, posture, and capability development to advance AI and machine learning (ML) technologies and about ways to counter the challenges China's aggressive pursuit of these technologies poses. For the purposes of this report, AI refers to the use of ML technologies to address a variety of application domains and problems, resulting in a multitude of capabilities, such as computer vision, natural-language processing, decision support, and command and control. ML is the field of computer science concerned with creating programs that "learn" from massive data sets using a large and evolving set of techniques grounded in statistics and mathematical optimization. For the sake of convenience, in this report, *AI* will be used to refer both to AI and ML.

Against this backdrop, in this report, we identify the aspects of AI that need whole-of-government attention to accelerate U.S. investment and implementation and the investments and policies that would support and protect AI growth in the U.S. commercial, academic, and government sectors. The goal would be for USAF to acquire a substantial military AI edge over its Chinese counterpart. We start by assessing current Chinese and U.S. AI strategies; investment levels; and the structural, systemic, and implementation differences that affect the development and adoption of AI in both nations. We then move on to examine the military implications of the

---

[1] State Council of the People's Republic of China, *A New Generation Artificial Intelligence Development Plan*, trans. Graham Webster, Rogier Creemers, Paul Triolo, and Elsa Kania, July 20, 2017.

[2] The White House, *National Security Strategy of the United States of America*, Washington, D.C., December 2017; James Mattis, *Summary of the 2018 National Defense Strategy of the United States of America: Sharpening the American Military's Competitive Edge*, Washington, D.C.: U.S. Department of Defense, 2018.

differences between the current U.S. and Chinese approaches to AI research and development (R&D).

Research Questions

The research was structured to address four main questions:

1. How do the U.S. and Chinese national strategies for AI compare?
2. What key differences in cultural and structural factors affect the implementation of U.S. and Chinese AI strategies?
3. How do these differences affect military capability development relevant to USAF?
4. How can USAF establish a competitive advantage in militarily relevant AI capabilities?

Methodology

The conclusions and recommendations of this report emerged from a comparative analysis of national AI strategies, cultural and structural factors, and military capability development. This comparative analysis was conducted through an examination of the relevant literature in English and Chinese. We surveyed five different literatures: the government AI planning literatures for both the United States and China, the academic science and technology (S&T) literature on AI trends and breakthroughs, the business literature on the financial ecosystems that support AI development in the United States and China, the literature on comparative cultural analysis across the United States and China, and the literature on the military science and operational concept implications of current AI technological developments.

This research represents a preliminary and necessarily limited approach to an extremely complex topic. While we have opted to survey primary source government reports and secondary source literature on the United States, China, and AI, we did not conduct or draw from extensive surveys of Chinese-language writings on AI and interviews with subject-matter experts in China and elsewhere. In part, this was because of time and resource limitations, but it also reflected the authors' sense that it would be difficult to obtain reliable and relevant information in China, given the highly sensitive nature of the topic. These additional approaches to data collection and analysis could be mined in follow-on research. Further research should provide a firm basis for either confirming or calling into question the preliminary findings of this research.

Then, to assess how the Air Force could maintain a competitive advance in AI, we developed a simple qualitative framework to help determine the appropriate allocation of USAF activities across the spectrum of AI research, development, and procurement. The framework assesses the level of effort that the USAF should undertake in each phase of the AI research, development, and procurement process.

Outline of This Report

Chapter 2 compares the national AI plans, cultures, and structures of China and the United States. Chapter 3 offers a menu of recommendations for the Air Force. Chapter 4 summarizes main conclusions and suggests fruitful avenues for future research on AI topics.

2. Comparing U.S.-China Artificial Intelligence Ecosystems

National Artificial Intelligence Strategies

Any viable national strategy must have clear goals, be properly resourced, and have appropriate mechanisms and methods, all under the direction of capable leadership.

China's National Artificial Intelligence Strategy

Leadership and Goals

China's national AI strategy was formulated at the behest of paramount political leader Xi Jinping, who is concurrently General Secretary of the Chinese Communist Party (CCP), chair of the People's Liberation Army (PLA)'s Central Military Commission, and president of the PRC. Xi has made AI a high priority. At the apex of leadership are the CCP politburo and the PRC State Council, while "comprehensive planning and coordination" is exercised by the National Science and Technology Structural Reform and Innovation System Construction Leading Small Group.[1] One of the most prominent figures in China, politburo member and State Council Deputy Premier Liu He, heads the Leading Small Group, but day-to-day leadership of the AI strategy is under Liu's deputy, Wang Zhigang, Minister of Science and Technology. Concurrently, Wang is head of the Artificial Intelligence Plan Implementation Office, which is also sited in the Ministry of Science and Technology.[2] The overarching goal of China's AI strategy is to create and sustain a national AI technology system, with an intelligent economy, an intelligent society, and a strengthened national defense in a three-step timeline:

- By 2020, China "will be in step with" world leaders in AI.
- By 2025, "China will achieve major breakthroughs in basic theories for AI."
- By 2030, China "should achieve world-leading levels."[3]

Mechanisms, Methods, Resources

The strategy has three key mechanisms, but the dominant one is **central planning**: China's AI strategy, launched in July 2017, is being implemented as a whole-of-regime (a CCP, PLA, and PRC effort) megamanaged campaign. To be effective, the strategy requires extensive **bureaucratic coordination**, both within the tripartite party-military-state regime and the AI

---

[1] "Organizational Leadership" in State Council of the People's Republic of China, 2017.

[2] State Council of the People's Republic of China, "State Council on the Adjustments to the National Science and Technology System Reform and Innovation System Construction Leading Small Group [国务院办公厅关于调整国家科技体制改革 和创新体系建设领导小组]," Guobanfa (2018), No. 86, September 7, 2018.

[3] "Strategic Objectives," in State Council of the People's Republic of China, 2017.

triangle of the state R&D structure, the military, and the commercial sector. The 29 members of the Leading Small Group represent a broad swath of PRC ministries, CCP central organs, and relevant PLA entities. A 27-person-strong advisory committee comprises leaders from academia, research institutes, and technology companies, along with two representatives from the PLA.[4]

The six distinct methods being pursued under the strategy are (1) domestic AI R&D efforts, (2) collaboration with PRC universities and state research institutes, (3) international investment, (4) mergers and acquisitions, (5) domestic and international recruitment of S&T personnel, and (6) theft and espionage.[5] The strategy seeks to leverage extensive resources, including vast quantities of consumer data, generous financing, ample hardware, China's sizeable R&D infrastructure, and the country's dynamic business community.

U.S. National Artificial Intelligence Strategy

Leadership and Goals

In May 2018, the White House released a fact sheet that outlined the high-priority AI programs across the government that are being funded.[6] The National Security Commission on Artificial Intelligence was established in the fiscal year 2019 National Defense Authorization Act.[7] The purpose and responsibilities of the commission are "to consider the methods and means necessary to advance the development of artificial intelligence, machine learning, and associated technologies to comprehensively address the national security and defense needs of the United States"[8] to better equip the nation with the means of addressing its national security needs, including economic risks, needs of DoD, and other security risks defined by the commission.

The Intelligence Community and DoD recently convened industry days for the commercial sector to articulate their unique needs and the technical gaps they are looking for industry to address. Both communities are standing up agencywide efforts to incorporate AI into their operations and leverage it for strategic advantage. The Intelligence Community has the Augmenting Intelligence with Machines program, and DoD has the Joint Artificial Intelligence Center.

---

[4] "Ministry of Science and Technology Announces its First 4 National New Generation A.I. Innovation Platforms, As Well As Its 27 Member Strategic Consultative Committee [科技部首批 4 家国家新一代人工智能开放创新平台, 27 位战略咨询委员会名单]," Sohu.com website, November 19, 2017.

[5] These six methods (or *models*) were identified in Daniel Alderman and Daniel Ray, "Artificial Intelligence, Emerging Technologies, and China-US Strategic Competition," in Tai Ming Cheung and Thomas G. Mahnken, eds., *The Gathering Pacific Storm: Emerging US-China Strategic Competition in Defense Technological and Industrial Development*, Amherst, N.Y.: Cambria Press, 2018, pp. 179–210.

[6] The White House, "Artificial Intelligence for the American People," fact sheet, May 10, 2018.

[7] Pub. L. 115-232, John S. McCain National Defense Authorization Act for Fiscal Year 2019, August 13, 2018.

[8] Pub. L. 115-232, 2018.

In September 2018, the Defense Advanced Research Projects Agency (DARPA) announced a $2 billion campaign to develop the next wave of AI technologies, supporting more than 20 programs that are exploring ways to advance the state of the art in AI, pushing beyond second-wave AI techniques toward contextual reasoning capabilities.[9]

Mechanisms, Methods, Resources

As of early 2020, the Networking, Information Technology, Research and Development National Coordination Office coordinates federally funded R&D in a number of information technology program areas, including intelligent robotics and autonomous systems.

In May 2016, the Obama administration called for increasing use of AI in government to improve services and benefit the American people.[10] The announcement explicitly recommended that the federal government explore ways to improve the capacity of key agencies to apply AI to their missions. It is not clear how these Barack Obama–era recommendations are being implemented under Donald Trump. While some have criticized the Trump administration for not providing sufficient focus or resources for AI development, President Trump did sign an executive order in early 2019 to spur AI development, and many government agencies have initiated their own programs to develop new AI applications.[11] To help maintain U.S. superiority in this area, DARPA is running a project called the Electronics Resurgence Initiative, which aims to develop new technologies to the point where they can be commercialized by private firms.[12] In 2018, the U.S. government stood up the Joint Artificial Intelligence Center with a budget and mandate to set up guardrails that set planning limits and define oversight and ethical boundaries. DoD has held annual AI industry days since 2017 to bring together private companies and military officials, allowing them to identify novel AI solutions to military problems.[13]

DARPA's Artificial Intelligence Exploration program, first announced in July 2018, constitutes a series of high-risk, high-payoff projects where researchers will work to establish the feasibility of new AI concepts within 18 months of award. This program is a key component of DARPA's AI Next campaign, a multiyear investment of more than $2 billion in new and existing programs whose purpose is to bolster U.S. capabilities in AI.[14] Previously, a U.S. national AI

[9] Sam Shead, "DARPA Plans to Spend $2 Billion Developing New AI Technologies," *Forbes*, September 7, 2018.

[10] Ed Felten, "Preparing for the Future of Artificial Intelligence," White House Office of Science and Technology Policy blog, May 3, 2016.

[11] Cade Metz, "Trump Signs Executive Order Promoting Artificial Intelligence," *New York Times,* February 11, 2019; Cade Metz, "As China Marches Forward on A.I., the White House Is Silent," *New York Times,* February 12, 2018.

[12] DARPA, "DARPA Electronics Resurgence Initiative," webpage, December 19, 2019.

[13] Loren Blinde, "Army to Host 3rd Annual DoD AI Industry Day," Intelligence Community News website, October 16, 2019.

[14] DARPA, "DARPA Announces $2 Billion Campaign to Develop Next Wave of AI Technologies," press release, September 7, 2018.

strategy had been articulated in *The National Artificial Intelligence Research and Development Strategic Plan*, released in October 2016 by the Obama administration's National Science and Technology Council.[15] In February 2019, the Trump administration issued what amounts to its own AI strategy: Executive Order 13859.[16] This relatively modest U.S. government attention to AI is in contrast to the tremendous resources that the U.S. private and academic sectors are focusing on AI. If the U.S. government can successfully leverage that investment, there is a much better chance for maintaining the U.S. technical advantage.

DoD support for AI R&D has a history dating back to the 1950s. Throughout its history, this support has played a crucial role in the development of the field. However, DoD support has not always been steadfast. It has ebbed and flowed, corresponding with periods of great expectations and excitement followed by periods of great disillusionment as a result of mismanagement of expectations. RAND colleagues have noted that the "history of AI is rife with mismanaged expectations and premature hype. We should be careful not to repeat that history."[17] Current DoD actions related to AI are dangerously headed toward repeating the errors of the past.[18]

Cultural and Structural Factors

Both culture and structure influence processes and outcomes in societies and organizations in the political, military, economic, and scientific spheres. A country's culture consists of the patterns of behavior and the values, norms, and beliefs of its inhabitants. It arises from historical experiences, traditions, and ideologies.[19] Organizations also possess their own distinct cultures, especially bureaucracies and armed forces.[20] Structure, meanwhile, consists of the arrangement

---

[15] National Science and Technology Council, *The National Artificial Intelligence Research and Development Strategic Plan*, Washington, D.C.: Executive Office of the President, October 2016.

[16] Executive Order 13859, *Maintaining American Leadership in Artificial Intelligence*, February 11, 2019; The White House, "Artificial Intelligence for the American People," website, February 19, 2019.

[17] For a detailed history and analysis, see Danielle C. Tarraf, William Shelton, Edward Parker, Brien Alkire, Diana Gehlhaus Carew, Justin Grana, Alexis Levedahl, Jasmin Léveillé, Jared Mondschein, James Ryseff, Ali Wyne, Dan Elinoff, Edward Geist, Benjamin N. Harris, Eric Hui, Cedric Kenney, Sydne Newberry, Chandler Sachs, Peter Schirmer, Danielle Schlang, Victoria Smith, Abbie Tingstad, Padmaja Vedula, and Kristin Warren, *The Department of Defense Posture for Artificial Intelligence: Assessment and Recommendations*, Santa Monica, Calif.: RAND Corporation, RR-4229-OSD, 2019.

[18] Tarraf et al., 2019.

[19] According to Clifford Geertz, one of the foremost scholars on the topic, culture is composed of "webs of significance." Geertz contends that humans are "suspended in [these] webs . . . [that humans themselves have] spun." Clifford Geertz, *The Interpretation of Cultures: Selected Essays*, New York: Basic Books, 1973, p. 5.

[20] James Q. Wilson, *Bureaucracy: What Government Agencies Do and Why They Do It*, New York: Basic Books, 1989. Also see Edgar H. Schein, "Coming to a New Awareness of Organizational Culture," *Sloan Management Review*, Vol. 25, No. 2, January 15, 1984, and S. Rebecca Zimmerman, Kimberly Jackson, Natasha Lander, Colin Roberts, Dan Madden, and Rebeca Orrie, *Movement and Maneuver: Culture and the Competition for Influence Among the U.S. Military Services*, Santa Monica, Calif.: RAND Corporation, RR-2270-OSD, 2019.

of and relations among the parts or elements of organizations and bureaucracies.[21] The following subsections outline the cultural and structural factors that will affect the processes and outcomes of the implementation of national AI strategies in China and in the United States, respectively.

Cultural Factors: China

History, Tradition, and Ideology

The Chinese are justifiably proud of being heirs to one of the world's oldest and most magnificent civilizations, with an impressive list of inventions. While China had a glorious distant past as a rich, powerful, and unified state, China was poor, weak, and frequently divided in more recent times. The CCP refers to a "Century of Humiliation" extending from the Opium Wars of the 1840s to the 1940s, when Japan occupied vast areas of China. According to the official narrative, the Chinese people were only able to stand up strong and united after the CCP and PLA defeated Japan and the corrupt Nationalist regime.[22] This official narrative is propaganda but is inculcated into citizens of the PRC via history textbooks to build up nationalism and bolster popular support for the CCP.[23]

Although, China has multiple philosophical and religious traditions, most scholars tend to emphasize Confucianism as an especially potent and enduring philosophy.[24] Confucianism, which has been a particularly influential tradition for successive generations of Chinese, emphasizes academic study, virtue, and harmonious social interactions. Although the CCP initially condemned Confucianism as backward and feudal, the CCP had rehabilitated this philosophy by the first decade of the 21st century and urged PRC citizens to live according to Confucian precepts.[25]

Although most of the 80 million CCP members pay only lip service to Marxism-Leninism, this ideology continues to exert a potent influence on contemporary China in fundamental ways. Regime leaders believe that the CCP possesses a superior scientific approach on all matters, including national security, economics, and S&T policy. Another ideological legacy is an abiding and deep sense of insecurity. CCP leaders perceive the existence of multiple internal and

---

[21] What James Wilson calls "the system of coordination" (Wilson, 1989, p. 24).

[22] Andrew Scobell, "China's Real Strategic Culture: A Great Wall of the Imagination," *Contemporary Security Policy,* Vol. 35, No. 2, August 2014.

[23] Zheng Wang, *Never Forget National Humiliation: Historical Memory in Chinese Politics and Foreign Relations,* New York: Columbia University Press, 2014.

[24] For a comprehensive overview of Chinese philosophy, see Benjamin I. Schwartz, *The World of Thought in Ancient China,* Cambridge, Mass.: Belknap Press of Harvard University, 1985. For an classic study of the influence of Confucianism on modern China, see Joseph R. Levenson, *Confucian China and Its Modern Fate,* in three volumes, Berkeley, Calif: University of California Press, 1958–1965.

[25] Scobell, 2014, p. 215. See also, Daniel A. Bell, *China's New Confucianism: Politics and Everyday Life in a Changing Society,* Princeton, N.J.: Princeton University Press, 2008.

external threats.[26] The primary goal of China's CCP leaders is to perpetuate the regime through long-term planning and implementing large projects.[27] Chinese leaders are especially enamored with S&T, possess a technonationalist outlook,[28] and perceive the United States to be China's greatest threat. They believe U.S. military dominance and economic preeminence are grounded in Washington's scientific and technological prowess, all of which is concentrated on containing and weakening CCP rule. China's top priority, therefore, is to counter this multidimensional threat, especially to overcome this S&T deficit.[29]

Society, Politics, Military, Research, and Business

PRC society has little trust, and most Chinese distrust fellow citizens unless they are family members, close friends, neighbors, classmates, or work colleagues.[30] In Chinese politics, power tends to be perceived in terms of status, and individual initiative or innovation is typically neither encouraged nor rewarded. In Chinese society, conservatism, conformity, and risk aversion are the norm.[31] Because power is primarily defined in terms of status and because distrust of subordinates tends to be high, PLA officers tend to prioritize status quo over change and control over command.[32] This low level of trust in subordinates in the military chain of command is starkly different from the U.S. military philosophy, which is grounded in the notion of empowering junior officers to take the initiative on the battlefield as long as they adhere to the broad guidance and direction their superiors give them. This principle of "centralized control, decentralized execution" appears to be anathema to most Chinese senior officers.

An overriding sense of cultural superiority pervades contemporary Chinese society in all endeavors. While the need for foreign know-how is recognized, the pervasive assumption is that China does not need to alter its fundamentals. Certainly, many Chinese appreciate that present-day China is far from perfect; some even consider traditional Chinese culture to be backward. These individuals believe that, for China to progress, traditional culture—or at least significant

---

[26] Andrew J. Nathan and Andrew Scobell, *China's Search for Security*, New York: Columbia University Press, 2012.

[27] Andrew Scobell, Edmund J. Burke, Cortez A. Cooper III, Sale Lilly, Chad J. R. Ohlandt, Eric Warner, and J. D. Williams, *China's Grand Strategy: Trends, Trajectories, Long-Term Competition*, Santa Monica, Calif.: RAND Corporation, RR-2798-A, forthcoming.

[28] Tai Ming Cheung, *Fortifying China: The Struggle to Build a Modern Defense Economy*, Ithaca, N.Y.: Cornell University Press, 2009, pp. 237–241.

[29] Scobell et al., forthcoming.

[30] Francis Fukuyama, *Trust: The Social Virtues and the Creation of Prosperity*, New York: Free Press, 1995, Ch. 8.

[31] On the PLA, see You Ji, *China's Military Transformation*, Cambridge, Mass.: Polity Press, 2016, pp. 20–21.

[32] An emphasis of control over command is a characteristic in the armed forces of Leninist party-states: This has been so thus far for the North Korean People's Army and is also true for the PLA. See Andrew Scobell and John Sanford, *North Korea's Military Threat: Pyongyang's Conventional Forces, Weapons of Mass Destruction, and Ballistic Missiles*, Carlisle Barracks, Pa.: U.S. Army War College Strategic Studies Institute, 2007, p. 10.

elements of it—must be abandoned.[33] Nevertheless, ethnocentrism and ethnonationalism are potent forces in Xi Jinping's China, even as the PRC has emerged as a wealthy and powerful country in the early 21st century.[34] Many Chinese are highly sensitive to criticism of their country's history and culture.[35] In Chinese culture writ large, there is a fear of failure and of the sense of shame that would accompany failure. This tends to produce a low tolerance for risk and fear of failure in a variety of settings, including in civilian S&T research.[36] A similar culture exists in China's military research, development, and acquisition systems.[37] However, some settings and organizations, by contrast, do tolerate higher levels of risk. This includes certain sectors of China's business community, such as venture capitalists, especially in the technology sector, in which, according to one knowledgeable individual, there is also a greater degree of individualism and flexibility, all in pursuit of profit.[38] Other sectors of the PRC economy, including state-owned enterprises appear to be somewhat more conservative and risk averse.[39]

Structural Factors: China

Certain characteristics of contemporary China's highly centralized governance structure can be traced back to past imperial dynasties, but the most relevant are organizations that were formed in the early and mid-20th century. China is a *party-state*, a classification that does not seem fully accurate because it omits a third major influential bureaucratic actor: the military. A more complete characterization of the regime is a **party-military-state**.[40] The most important organization is the CCP, established in 1921, with the second most important organization being

---

[33] This critical view of traditional Chinese culture has been an enduring strand in successive generations of Chinese reformers and revolutionaries, including the leaders of the CCP.

[34] Xi Jinping's China Dream of national rejuvenation resonates with most Chinese people, who take tremendous pride in both China's contemporary accomplishments and its past glories and traditions.

[35] One of the authors has drawn a parallel with the way many Americans view the origins and principles of their system of government, as enshrined in such documents as the Declaration of Independence and the U.S. Constitution: Andrew Scobell, *China's Use of Military Force: Beyond the Great Wall and the Long March,* New York: Cambridge University Press, 2003, p. 27.

[36] Denis Fred Simon and Cong Cao, *China's Emerging Technological Edge: Assessing the Role of High-End Talent,* New York: Cambridge University Press, 2009, p. 21.

[37] Tai Ming Cheung, Thomas G. Mahnken, and Andrew L. Ross, "Frameworks for Analyzing Chinese Defense and Military Innovation," in Tai Ming Cheung, *Forging China's Military Might: A New Framework for Assessing Innovation,* Baltimore, Md.: Johns Hopkins University Press, 2014, p. 25.

[38] Kai-Fu Lee, *AI Superpowers: China, Silicon Valley and the New World Order*, Boston: Houghton Mifflin Harcourt, 2018, pp. 25–27.

[39] Irene Hau-Siu Chow, "The Relationship Between Entrepreneurial Orientation and Firm Performance in China," *SAM Advanced Management Journal,* Vol. 71, No. 3, Summer 2006. Nevertheless, this conservatism and degree of autonomy fluctuates depending on the degree of state control over a particular state-owned enterprise. See William J. Norris, *Chinese Economic Statecraft: Commercial Actors, Grand Strategy, and State Control*, Ithaca, N.Y.: Cornell University Press, 2016.

[40] Nathan and Scobell, 2012, p. 57; Scobell et al., forthcoming, pp. 17–18.

the PLA, established six years later. The state organization, the PRC, was not formally founded until 1949.

Since 1978, during the post-Mao period of economic reform, the PLA has withdrawn from governance, largely removed itself from the rough and tumble of politics, and formed a more insular bureaucratic system, functioning largely separately from the CCP and PRC bureaucracies.[41] Yet the three bureaucratic systems are fused at the top in the figure of a paramount leader—currently Xi Jinping—who exercises control over the entire tripartite system.[42] Moreover, the CCP penetrates the PLA at all levels via a system of political commissars and party committees and because all military officers are also CCP members. The CCP also penetrates the entire civilian PRC apparatus.[43]

China's Leninist tripartite bureaucratic structure is highly centralized and top down. Thus, when a decision is made or a policy launched, execution can swiftly follow. While central planning is a hallmark of communist party–military states, this rarely means smooth bureaucratic coordination or 100 percent compliance in implementation. In recognition of this challenge, a high-powered small leading group staffed with senior officials from different bureaucracies is charged with overseeing China's AI strategy.[44]

Officially, civil-military fusion is much hyped. While there are fewer legal and ethical barriers to the sharing of technology developed in the civilian and commercial worlds with the military world, the PLA tends to be an insular and distinct bureaucratic system, especially in the research, development, and acquisition system.[45] This system is "compartmentalized" and "suffers from bureaucratic fragmentation."[46] While China possesses a vast reservoir of data and there are few formal barriers to sharing it, there is a culture of secrecy, especially within military bureaucracies. Thus, interaction, coordination, and cooperation between the military and civilian entities are not as simple or easy as they might appear from the outside.

---

[41] One prominent scholar dubs the PLA "a state within a state." Kenneth Lieberthal, *Governing China: From Revolution Through Reform,* 2nd ed. New York: W.W. Norton, 2004, p. 230.

[42] Nathan and Scobell, 2012, pp. 37–38, 41–46.

[43] Nathan and Scobell, 2012, pp. 39–41; Lieberthal, 2004, Chs. 6 and 7.

[44] On leading small groups, see Nathan and Scobell, 2012, pp. 48–50, and Lieberthal, 2004, pp. 215–218.

[45] Cheung, Mahnken, and Ross, 2014, p. 25.

[46] Tai Ming Cheung, "An Uncertain Transition: Regulatory Reform and Industrial Innovation in China's Defense Research, Development and Acquisition System," in Tai Ming Cheung, *Forging China's Military Might: A New Framework for Assessing Innovation,* Baltimore, Md.: Johns Hopkins University Press, 2014a, pp. 52, 53. See also Chapter Six of Michael S. Chase, Jeffrey Engstrom, Tai Ming Cheung, Kristen A. Gunness, Scott Warren Harold, Susan Puska, and Samuel K. Berkowitz, *China's Incomplete Military Transformation: Assessing the Weaknesses of People's Liberation Army (PLA),* Santa Monica, Calif.: RAND Corporation, RR-893-USCC, 2015.

Cultural Factors: United States

History, Tradition, and Ideology

Although, compared with China, the United States has had a relatively short existence as a political and cultural entity, the dominant narrative is one of dramatic economic growth, territorial expansion, and technological progress, combined with relative political stability during its nearly 250 years of history. The United States has a sense of destiny, believing that it serves as a beacon of inspiration to the world and a global force for good—in other words a sense of national superiority. Americans say their country is open, egalitarian, and innovative. Most Americans hold great reverence for their own political institutions and ideals, as embodied in such documents as the Declaration of Independence and Constitution.[47] Although ongoing partisan feuding in Washington, D.C., and enduring inequalities around the country have disillusioned or even alienated many Americans, most continue to hold onto the American Dream, a belief that hard work and individual initiative will be rewarded.[48] While Americans would not consider themselves *ideological*, if the term means modes of thinking, the United States does possess an *ideology*: an optimistic belief that Americans live in a land of opportunity and that every problem has a solution.[49] This ideology also includes a conviction in political freedoms, a free-enterprise system, and confidence that technology will improve the people's lives.[50]

Society, Politics, Military, Research, and Business

The United States is a high-trust society, and most Americans tend to trust fellow citizens, although there are periodic crises of trust in U.S. political institutions.[51] Status is generally less important in American organizations, and hierarchies are flatter.[52] The U.S. military is mission oriented, and superiors tend to permit their subordinates considerable initiative. In R&D, initiative and innovation are valued and usually rewarded, and there is significant occupational and geographic mobility. Although U.S. business is highly competitive and focused on profit,

---

[47] On the power of a core U.S. ideal and its messy historical reality, see Eric Foner, *The Story of American Freedom*, New York: Norton, 1999.

[48] See, for example, Robert D. Putnam, *Our Kids: The American Dream in Crisis*, New York: Simon and Schuster, 2015.

[49] This is according to public opinion polling. See, for example, Samantha Smith, "Most Think the 'American Dream' Is Within Reach for Them," Pew Research Center website, October 31, 2017.

[50] Kai-Fu Lee comments on this characteristic (Lee, 2018, p. 26).

[51] Fukuyama, 1995, Pt. IV.

[52] Unlike Americans, Chinese tend to conceive of power in terms of status. Helen Spencer-Oatey, "Unequal Relationships in High and Low Power Distance Societies: A Comparative Study of Tutor-Student Role Relations in Britain and China," *Journal of Cross-Cultural Psychology,* Vol. 28, No. 3, May 1997, pp. 284–286; Weipeng Ling, Lei Wang, and Shuting Chen, "Abusive Supervision and Employee Well-Being: The Moderating Effect of Power Distance Orientation," *Applied Psychology,* Vol. 62, No. 2, 2013, pp. 312–313, 323.

innovation and trendiness are often valued in the technology sector over whether an idea or product can be mass marketed. According to Bill Gates, Microsoft's

> corporate culture nurtures an atmosphere in which creative thinking thrives, and employees develop to their fullest potential. . . . Our strategy has always been to hire strong, creative employees, and delegate responsibility and resources to them so they can get the job done.[53]

The culture of Silicon Valley is mission driven, focused on the task at hand.[54] Many tech entrepreneurs feel strongly that regulation by and cooperation with the government are antithetical to their companies' ethos. Technology companies are often deeply reluctant to engage with the U.S. national security apparatus because doing so raises issues of privacy and government interference.[55]

Structural Factors: United States

The U.S. political system is characterized by a diffusion of power among separate branches of government. The existence of a two-party system, three differentiated branches of the national government, and 50 autonomous state governments creates a system of checks and balances that can make it quite challenging for the executive branch to formulate and execute national-level policies.

There is an institutionalized federally supported R&D structure with longstanding relationships and linkages between research institutes, universities, national laboratories, defense contractors, and DoD. During the Cold War, the federal government undertook a massive mobilization of the U.S. scientific R&D community, in the interest of national security.[56] Earlier generations of defense technologies were spun off to the commercial technology sector and became ubiquitous in U.S. society. With AI, the situation is inverted: Tech companies are pioneering the R&D of AI, while the U.S. government seeks to leverage this technology for national security purposes.[57]

---

[53] Geoffrey James, "Bill Gates Told Me This 25 Years Ago and It's Still Freakin' Brilliant," *Inc.*, September 17, 2019. The original quote appeared in Geoffrey James, *Business Wisdom of the Electronic Elite*, New York: Random House, 1996.

[54] Kai-Fu Lee, 2018, p. 26.

[55] Daniel S. Hoadley and Nathan J. Lucas, *Artificial Intelligence and National Security*, Washington, D.C.: Congressional Research Service, April 26, 2018, pp. 7–8.

[56] The technology initiative was critical to successful U.S. competition with the Soviet Union. See William H. McNeill, *The Pursuit of Power*, Chicago: University of Chicago Press, 1982, pp. 368–369.

[57] Hoadley and Lucas, 2018, p. 13.

Bottom Line: How Do They Compare?

Comparing National AI Plans

Both countries have articulated extremely ambitious strategies that will not be easy to deliver on. China might have the edge in terms of continuity of leadership and its whole-of-regime approach, which permits an impressive concentration of resources and focus of effort that play to the regime's perceived advantages in pursuit of what it considers major undertakings.[58] The PRC's top-down Leninist system has proved adept at mobilizing extensive resources in pursuit of ambitious national goals. The campaigns Beijing has launched have been hallmarks of both the Maoist and post-Mao eras.[59] Which country can attain more of its goals will depend on whether China can grasp its perceived first-mover advantage or the United States can leverage its position of world leadership.[60] Moreover, each country will have to overcome the same two daunting challenges. The first challenge is establishing and then sustaining the level of coordination required both among a myriad of government bureaucracies and among government entities, commercial actors, and academia. China may have a slight edge when it comes to harnessing the dynamism of its commercial tech sector, but the United States may have the edge when it comes to the application of AI technology to military operations. A second challenge for each country will be maintaining focus: AI technology is prone to distractions and diversions. There is no commonly agreed on definition of AI, and it is hard to get concrete about AI. As a result, AI tends to be conceived of in very abstract terms, making focused research and measuring progress very difficult. This challenge may be surmountable in China, at least in AI areas that have been prioritized. And it may be surmountable in basic research in America, where the U.S. government has a history of committing to "sustained fundamental research efforts" that take decades to show results.[61]

Comparing Culture

Overall, cultural factors tend to favor the United States when it comes to the likelihood of successfully executing a national AI strategy. First, implementing an AI strategy is much smoother in a result-oriented high-trust society than in a status-conscious low-trust one. Second, in terms of ease of military application, AI is simpler to integrate into a military culture that

---

[58] "Basic Principles" in State Council of the People's Republic of China, 2017.

[59] Elizabeth J. Perry, "From Mass Campaigns to Managed Campaigns: 'Constructing a New Socialist Countryside,'" in Sebastian Heilmann and Elizabeth J. Perry, eds., *Mao's Invisible Hand: The Political Foundations of Adaptive Governance in China*, Cambridge, Mass: Harvard University Asia Center, 2011.

[60] "Introduction" in State Council of the People's Republic of China, 2017; National Science and Technology Council, *The National Artificial Intelligence Research and Development Strategic Plan*, Washington, D.C.: Executive Office of the President, June 2019. See also the discussion in Lee, 2018, pp. 14–17.

[61] "AI R&D Strategy " in National Science and Technology Council, 2019.

accepts risk and in which superiors balance attention to command and to control than into one that is averse to risk and in which superiors are more intent on controlling subordinates than on commanding them. Third, among scientists and technical research personnel, U.S. R&D culture encourages initiative and innovation, but Chinese culture tends to dampen such instincts and discourage such actions. Fourth, the U.S. system has clear processes of verification, validation, test, and evaluation (VVT&E), while these processes are less clear in China. Fifth, China's AI strategy has generous financing but suffers from the corruption endemic in Chinese society. Although funding is less plentiful in the United States, a culture of strict monitoring and fiscal oversight means that whatever financing is available is less likely to be wasted.

Cross-national comparisons of a qualitative concept, such as culture, are fraught with controversy. Such scholarship is prone to criticisms of stereotyping and bias. Culture is a notoriously difficult concept to define and measure. This makes comparing cultures particularly challenging. Yet most scholars agree that culture is an important variable that influences how individuals act, whether in politics, military affairs, business, or scientific research.[62] Individuals are influenced by their experiences and their immediate environment. Not only is an individual's immediate context important, but the overall cultural milieu is also extremely important. While the microenvironment cannot be overlooked, the macroenvironment is arguably a more and more pervasive overarching influence. This includes the influences of history, tradition, and ideology on national culture, which is inculcated through childrearing and education. That culture is a key factor in China is widely accepted by the academic community.[63]

The work of Geert Hofstede, a prominent European scholar and consultant on the issue of national cross-cultural comparison, provides some valuable insights into macrolevel cultural differences between China and the United States that support our assessments. His research and conclusions, particularly his quantitative approach to measuring cultural differences, have been shown to be both useful and consistent with other research on cultural difference.[64] Hofstede developed a multidimensional model for the systematic comparison of national cultures based on research conducted within a large multinational technology corporation among employees located in a wide range of countries. This model compares national cultures in terms of:

---

[62] For example, Lucian Pye highlights the importance of national cultural differences for politicians: "Could a Boston 'pol' make it in Charleston, South Carolina, to say nothing of Tokyo?" (Lucian W. Pye, *Asian Power and Politics: The Cultural Dimensions of Authority*, Cambridge, Mass: Belknap Press, 1985, p. ix). Separating out the matter of language, a fundamental fact is that political leaders act quite differently in different countries, even while performing the same basic functions.

[63] Of course, while there is widespread agreement on the importance of culture, there is considerable debate on the actual effects of culture and how to measure them.

[64] Geert Hofstede, *Culture's Consequences: Comparing Values, Behaviors, Institutions, and Organizations Across Nations*, 2nd ed., Thousand Oaks, Calif.: Sage Publications, 2001. See also Geert Hofstede and Gert Jan Hofstede, *Cultures and Organizations: Software of the Mind*, 2nd ed., New York: McGraw-Hill, 2005; and the Geert Hofstede website, undated. For a critique, see Michael L. Jones, "Hofstede—Culturally Questionable?" paper presented at the 2007 Oxford Business and Economics Conference, Oxford, UK, June 24–26, 2007.

individualism, power distance, masculinity (use of force), uncertainty avoidance, long-term orientation, and indulgence. Most of these terms are self-explanatory; a few are not. *Power distance* has to do with how well the less-empowered members of the society accept the power imbalances in the culture that work against them. *Masculinity* refers to the level of cultural tolerance in a society for the use of force. Finally, *indulgence* has to do with a society's acceptance and promotion of leisure activities and the consumption of luxury goods.

Hofstede has measured his six variables for both the United States and China. His analysis found that the United States is far more individualistic than China and that the United States is also slightly higher in terms of uncertainty avoidance. In the category of indulgence, the United States is far ahead of China in terms of cultural acceptance. More-recent survey research in China among entrepreneurs supports Hofstede's analysis.[65] Chinese culture leads in the power distance and long-term orientation categories by wide margins, while the two countries are very close in terms of their acceptance of the use of force. All this seems to reinforce, in broad terms, our qualitative cultural analysis in this research. The U.S. lead in individualism and the fact that U.S. culture is less prone to accept existing power relationships bode well for the U.S. future in AI development because success in AI is going to be correlated with freewheeling small companies in which there is little structure; junior employees are empowered to bring new ideas to senior executives; and individual entrepreneurship is highly valued. The higher U.S. score in uncertainty avoidance is also a positive, implying that American engineers and scientists working in AI will be more dedicated to achieving clear solutions to problems as quickly as possible. The bad news for the United States from Hofstede's work is that China has a much higher score in long-term orientation, which implies that the Chinese will be taking the long view in the AI race and will probably approach the race more systematically and with more national resources than will the United States. The Chinese will also likely not be deterred by any early lead that the United States might achieve in the AI competition and will likely continue to wage this competition for decades, if that is what they perceive to be necessary to achieve a strong global power status.

Comparing Structure

Overall, structure does not tend to favor one country over the other. When it comes to the implementation of China's AI strategy, the regime's highly centralized Leninist system might seem to have the edge, but this is counteracted by severe bureaucratic stovepiping. Although the United States is relatively decentralized politically, an interagency coordination system may help offset this apparent Chinese advantage. In terms of military application of AI, China once again appears to have the advantage. Civil-military fusion is strongly emphasized, but the PLA's insular set of bureaucratic systems tends to make that fusion challenging. Some U.S. AI

---

[65] See for example, Bruce J. Dickson, *Wealth into Power: The Communist Party's Embrace of China's Private Sector*, New York: Cambridge University Press, 2008.

companies stymie the government by refusing to cooperate with it for ethical reasons, although many other companies are eager to land defense or government contracts.[66] As for data, China would also seem to have the edge. China has few legal or ethical barriers to sharing data, but a pervasive culture of secrecy counteracts this apparent advantage. China is a low-trust society, and stovepiping is a serious problem in PRC bureaucracy, so sharing information and data is not a simple or normal activity.[67] The United States has notable legal and ethical barriers to widespread sharing of data.

Conclusions and Wrap Up

S&T innovation faces significant cultural and structural barriers in China. Nevertheless, the top echelon of political leadership is aware of many of these impediments and is working to surmount them through several major ongoing initiatives. Foremost among these is the thoroughgoing organizational reform of China's national defense system that Xi Jinping launched in 2015.[68] The overarching goal of this effort is to produce a more streamlined structure with forces capable of waging joint campaigns of informatized warfare equipped with effective high-technology weapon systems researched, developed, tested, evaluated, and built in China.

Fostering cultures and forging structures in which innovation can thrive remains challenging in contemporary China. Outside China's robust venture capital technology sector of the business community,[69] culture and structure in the PRC are not particularly conducive to technological innovation. It may be more feasible to create one or more regional innovation systems within China—or with the Chinese diaspora, including Singapore and Taiwan—in which bureaucratic coordination challenges are more likely to be surmounted, collaboration efforts to be fruitful, and focus to be sustained.[70]

Although U.S. culture and structures pose challenges to technological innovation in AI, these mostly constitute advantages for the United States on balance. Leveraging the national security–related scientific R&D system established during the Cold War, such as the network of national

---

[66] Note, for example, Google's decision to cancel its Project Maven contract with DoD and Apple's consistent refusal to decrypt its iPhones for the Department of Justice. That being said, other companies, such as IBM, Microsoft, and Amazon, proactively seek out government contracts. See Jack Nicas and Katie Benner, "F.B.I. Asks Apple to Help Unlock Two iPhones," *New York Times,* January 7, 2020; Daisuke Wakabayashi and Scott Shane, "Google Will Not Renew Pentagon Contract That Upset Employees," *New York Times,* June 1, 2018.

[67] Fukuyama, 1995; Elsa B. Kania, "Chinese Military Innovation in Artificial Intelligence," testimony before the U.S.-China Economic and Security Review Commission Hearing on Trade, Technology, and Military-Civil Fusion, June 7, 2019.

[68] For a midcourse assessment, see Joel Wuthnow and Phillip C. Saunders, Chinese *Military Reforms in the Age of Xi Jinping: Drivers, Challenges and Implications*, Washington, D.C.: National Defense University Press, 2017.

[69] Lee, 2018.

[70] On regional innovation systems, see Henry S. Rowan, Marguerite Gong Hancock, and William F. Miller, eds., *Greater China's Quest for Innovation*, Stanford, Calif.: Walter H. Shorenstein Asia-Pacific Research Center, 2008, pp. 309–356.

laboratories, and developing new structures to engage with the cutting-edge commercial AI sector seem advisable.

3. Recommendations

Axes of Competition

Transforming AI advances into military capabilities requires leveraging advances in fundamental research or commercial industry, transitioning them to the military, assessing their effectiveness and suitability, and updating existing operational concepts or developing new ones to take advantage of the newly developed capabilities. We thus assessed the potential for U.S.-China competition in AI along five main axes: breakthrough fundamental research, advances in commercial industry, development and engineering to transition AI to the military, advances in VVT&E, and operational concept development.

What Is Not an Axis of Competition, and Why Not?

Our analyses indicate that breakthrough fundamental research is unlikely to be the basis of successful U.S. competition against China. Indeed, basic research results are driven primarily by academia and commercial industry; are typically published in the open literature; and are, thus, typically accessible worldwide. Moreover, China is increasingly fostering avenues for collaboration among Chinese and foreign academics, including Chinese scientists with direct ties to the PLA (see Figure 3.1), leading to a significant increase in joint publications (Figure 3.2). Finally, many prominent scientists in the field appear to have close ties with both the United States and China.

Advances in commercial industry are also unlikely to be the basis of successful U.S. competition against China. Indeed, China may hold an advantage there because of the tight integration between Chinese industry and Chinese military interests, made possible by the favorable structural factors in China. Moreover, until 2017, U.S. and Chinese investments had become increasingly entangled, with U.S. and Chinese backing of cross-border startups on the rise (Table 3.1). Furthermore, technology transfer is extremely difficult to control in practice when it does not involve the export of physical goods, as might be the case with AI-based technologies. Nevertheless, escalating great-power competition has produced escalating economic and technological competition between the United States and China. As a result, PRC foreign direct investment in the United States has dropped dramatically since 2016, from $46.5 billion to $5.4 billion.[1] This has been accompanied by considerable talk of the two countries "decoupling" their economies. Although this is unlikely to sever all economic ties

---

[1] Yusuf Khan, "Chinese Investment into the US Has Plunged 90% Since Trump Took Office—and Poorer States May Get Hit the Hardest," Business Insider website, July 22, 2019.

Figure 3.1. Top 10 Countries Having Collaborations with People's Liberation Army Scientists as Measured by Number of Jointly Authored Peer-Reviewed Articles

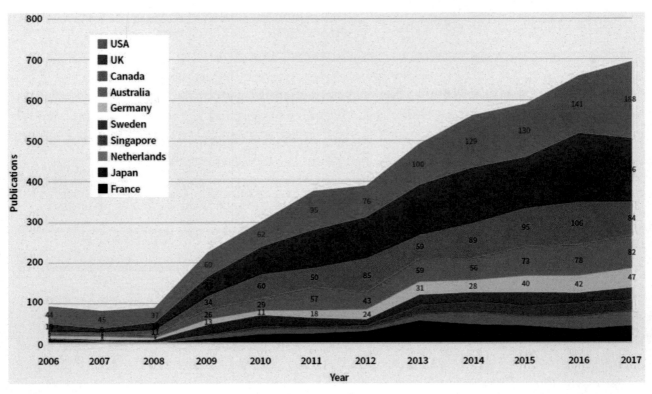

SOURCE: Alex Joske, *Picking Flowers, Making Honey: The Chinese Military's Collaboration with Foreign Universities*, Canberra: International Cyber Policy Center, Australian Strategic Policy Institute, 2018, p. 8. Used with permission.

Figure 3.2. Peer-Reviewed Articles Coauthored by People's Liberation Army Scientists and Overseas Scientists

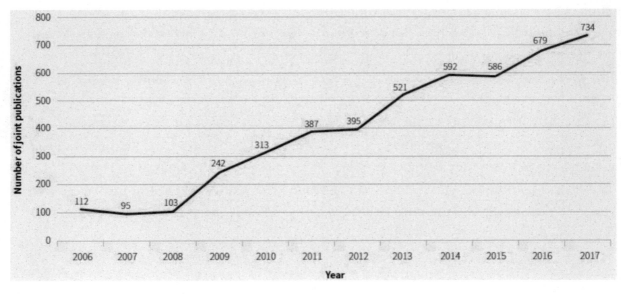

SOURCE: Joske, 2018, p. 4. Used with permission.

**Table 3.1. Prior Growth of Cross-Border Investments
in Artificial Intelligence, 2013–2017**

Year	China-Backed Equity Deals to U.S. Startups	U.S.-Backed Equity Deals to Chinese Startups
2013	1	1
2014	6	4
2015	14	3
2016	19	5
2017	31	20

SOURCE: CB Insights, "Top AI Trends to Watch in 2018," New York, 2018.

between the United States and China, it is likely to significantly affect tech companies and disrupt global supply chains.[2] In short, the trend of U.S.-China AI investment entanglement has been reversed.

What Are the Axes of Competition, and How Do We Assess the Current AI Balance?

The remaining three axes are thus potential avenues for the United States to establish and maintain a competitive edge. Additionally, as the two previous AI winters—periods of reduced funding and interest in AI research[3]—have demonstrated, managing expectations is an important aspect of ensuring steady technological advancement and effective adoption, particularly in the midst of hype. In what follows, we outline specific recommendations for each of these axes, starting with the critical issue of expectation management.

Manage Expectations

Realistic expectations are critical to successfully sustaining a program whose goal is to apply any new technology. This is a particularly sensitive issue for technologies, such as AI, that are the subject of grossly exaggerated and nonstop coverage in the media. Oren Etzioni, chief executive of the Allen Institute of Artificial Intelligence and an expert in the field, recently cautioned that "given the excitement and investment in deep learning, it's important to analyze it and consider [its] limitations."[4] The lack of clarity about the current capabilities and limitations of AI technologies may doom any attempt to incorporate them into useful systems. The United

---

[2] Simina Mistreanu "Beyond 'Decoupling': How China Will Reshape Global Trade in 2020," *Forbes*, December 3, 2019.

[3] For a definition of *AI winter*, see Jocelyn Paine, "W is for Winter," *AI Expert Newsletter*, January 2005. Many well-researched and comprehensive histories of AI are available that include discussion of past AI winters. See, for example, Daniel Crevier, *AI: The Tumultuous History of the Search for Artificial Intelligence*, Basic Books, 1993, and Alex Roland and Philip Shiman, *Strategic Computing: DARPA and the Quest for Machine Intelligence, 1983–1993*, MIT Press, 2002.

[4] Quoted in Richard Waters, "Why We Are in Danger of Overestimating AI," *Financial Times*, February 5, 2018.

States must exercise great care and caution to make sure this does not happen because AI technologies, beyond all the hype, have a great deal to offer, both today and in the future, even if AI is not the stuff of science fiction portrayed in the media.

To help keep USAF AI efforts achievable and on a solid footing, we recommend creating a forward-looking AI roadmap. We further recommend that the creation and maintenance of the roadmap be the responsibility of the AI cross-functional team the Air Force created in 2018, which draws on expertise from all major USAF commands, giving it a balanced perspective on realistic goals for AI employment for various time horizons. This AI roadmap should be organized according to three periods: the near (one to two years), medium (three to five years), and long (six to ten years) terms. The roadmap should

- contain a detailed and prioritized list of applications that are likely to be achievable in each period
- for each application, identify an operational need
- for each application, provide a plan for transition to operations, including test and evaluation
- for each application, list shortfalls in the current arsenal of AI technologies that would need to be developed to bring it to maturity when planned
- for each shortfall identified, suggest possible approaches, explaining why they could succeed
- for each shortfall identified, note the needed R&D, which could serve as the basis of calls for proposals
- for each application, offer a rough-order-of-magnitude estimate of the total cost to bring the application to maturity.

The AI roadmap should be a dynamic and living document that must be constantly maintained and revised as Air Force operational requirements and technology evolve. If done properly, the roadmap, Air Force operational requirements, and R&D requirements will coevolve. The roadmap, as we envision it, is a dynamic tool that will prevent Air Force equipment modernization and recapitalization planning from getting too far ahead of the pace of the application growth the USAF R&D community provides. If employed correctly, the roadmap could save the USAF from squandering precious acquisition funds on concepts that are not achievable with current AI applications.

Creating an effective AI roadmap will require a historical and technical perspective. Michael Jordan, professor of computer science at the University of California at Berkeley, makes an important distinction between *human-imitative AI*, which refers to "the heady aspiration of realizing in software and hardware an entity possessing human-level intelligence," and *intelligence augmentation*, which refers to a type of engineering in which "computation and data are used to create services that augment human intelligence and creativity."[5] Search engines and natural-language translation are good examples of intelligence augmentation. The past 20 years

---

[5] Michael Jordan, "Artificial Intelligence—the Revolution Hasn't Happened Yet," Medium website, April 19, 2018.

have seen remarkable progress in intelligence augmentation ushering in what amounts to a new branch of engineering founded on developments in "ideas such as 'information,' 'algorithm,' 'data,' 'uncertainty,' 'computing,' 'inference,' and 'optimization.'"[6] This is analogous to the way the field of chemical engineering is founded on developments in physics and chemistry.

The distinction between human-imitative AI and intelligence augmentation as an engineering discipline will help separate fanciful discussions of AI from the engineering realities of intelligence augmentation. In particular, it will help engineers base their efforts on sound, established principles that demand careful and sober examination of what is and is not feasible and how developments can be quantifiably validated, tested, and incorporated into other engineering systems. It will help the Air Force focus on evolutionary progress instead of expecting breakthrough revolutions.

A common perception is that we are currently experiencing what might be called a golden age of AI research. Many quantitative measures support this sentiment, including the growth of AI publications, attendance at major conferences, and overall investment in AI. However, there are also some negative trends. In fact, the sheer pace of growth of AI, especially deep learning,[7] has caused many to worry that there might be an AI bubble because the growth does not match the actual progress. AI research has historically experienced numerous periods of decreased progress, funding, and enthusiasm. These AI winters must be avoided by clear vision that is not clouded by media hype.

Create an Engineering Pipeline Under DoD Control

To establish and maintain a competitive edge in AI development and application, USAF and DoD will need large numbers of highly trained engineers. DoD engineers need to work in continuous and close cooperation with DoD program managers, operators, and data to

1. analyze requirements
2. develop design, test, and evaluation techniques for AI-warfare operational concepts
3. engineer DoD-specific AI systems
4. conduct VVT&E of DoD AI systems from laboratory to field.

Building and maintaining such a workforce has proven difficult, particularly given the high salaries and superior equipment offered in the private sector. The current DoD civilian engineering workforce is talented but contains a relatively small number of researchers skilled in

---

[6] Jordan, 2018.

[7] Gary Marcus, "Deep Learning: A Critical Appraisal," paper, undated.

the information technology–related disciplines needed for AI development.[8] It is also relatively old, with about one-third of DoD civilian engineers eligible to retire within the next five years.[9]

While the problem is significant, the Air Force and DoD can take measures that will help ensure that the U.S. military has the minds it needs to stay at the forefront of AI research and application. First, DoD can offer engineers more-flexible career paths, with opportunities to leave DoD laboratories and then return without prohibitive penalties; salaries based on performance, not just seniority; and the opportunity to continue conducting research, instead of being forced into management at a certain level of seniority. DoD engineers could receive more professional development opportunities, with opportunities to attend conferences, publish papers, and perhaps work on internally funded personal research. Finally, greater funds should be allocated from the military construction budget to update the old and aging laboratory equipment in many DoD labs.

The Air Force could also take steps to attract more AI engineers into its uniformed ranks. An AI Air National Guard Corps could be established to give midcareer AI researchers the opportunity to work part time in DoD labs and to enter the military at a rank commensurate with their experience. AI ROTC programs could also be founded at major AI universities, such as the Massachusetts Institute of Technology or Carnegie Mellon University, to attract young engineers in training into military research. Those who participate in these programs should be given AI engineering specialist career tracks and bonuses to secure a sufficient number of sufficiently skilled students. Finally, the Air Force can encourage students at its professional military education institutions to study AI applications so that, when they are promoted to leadership positions, they will be knowledgeable about AI techniques and capabilities and able to use these capabilities effectively in their future commands.

Create and Tailor Verification, Validation, Test, and Evaluation Techniques for Artificial Intelligence Technologies

Recommendations for Verification and Validation

Verification and *validation* refer to two distinct approaches for collectively assessing the quality of an AI system by checking that it meets its specifications (verification) and fulfills its intended purpose (validation). To frame reasonable verification and validation requirements, it may be appropriate to consider how an AI system might fall short. A 2016 paper investigated the

---

[8] See Gilbert Decker, Robert A. Beaudet, Siddhartha Dalal, Jay Davis, William H. Forster, George T. Singley III, David E. Mosher, Caroline Reilly, Phil Kehres, Gary Cecchine, and Nicholas C. Maynard, *Improving Army Basic Research: Report of an Expert Panel on the Future of Army Laboratories*, Santa Monica, Calif.: RAND Corporation, MG-1176-A, 2012, p. 16.

[9] Aileen Sedmak, Office of the DASD (Systems Engineering), "Understanding the DoD's Engineering Workforce," briefing delivered at NDIA Systems Engineering Conference, October 29, 2015, slide 11.

question of AI safety, framing it in the context of five research problems that highlight different points in the design process where things can go wrong:[10]

- *Avoiding side effects*—AI systems can be single-minded in pursuing their objective, sometimes causing problems in other areas not immediately relevant to it. Amodei et al. gave the example of a cleaning robot that rushes to clean as quickly as possible (its objective) and, in the process, knocks things over. These problems can be addressed by building a careful, nuanced objective function.
- *Avoiding reward hacking*—AI systems sometimes find shortcuts to fulfill their objective function that produce useless or destructive behavior. For example, Amodei et al. noted that a cleaning robot with the objective of cleaning all dirt it can see may fulfill this objective by switching off its sensor. As with avoiding side effects, this problem can be addressed by properly defining an objective function.
- *Scalable supervision*—While an overly simplistic objective function may lead to negative side effects or reward hacking, one that is too complex or that takes too long to evaluate may make it difficult for an AI system to assess courses of action. Returning to the hypothetical cleaning system, a scalable supervision problem might be a need for a cleaning robot to ask every family member whether any object found on the floor is theirs. While this would prevent the system from throwing away anyone's property, it would also potentially make cleaning the floor prohibitively time consuming.
- *Safe exploration*—Because an AI system learns by trial and error, it should be prevented from attempting trials that are exceptionally dangerous. For Amodei et al.'s cleaning robot, this could include instructions to never use wet mops near electrical equipment as it is experimenting with new cleaning techniques.
- *Robustness to distributional shift*—If the real-world information or environment an AI system encounters is significantly different from the data or environment it was trained on, its behavior may be suboptimal or even damaging. To illustrate, Amodei et al. noted that a robot trained to clean a factory floor may learn behaviors that would be unwise to use in a home, such as using a pressure washer on walls not built for such tools. Designers should proceed with great caution if the real-world environment is likely to be statistically different from the training environment.

Addressing the first two concerns fall under the auspices of validation, while addressing the last three falls under verification.

Verification and validation for AI systems, while still in its infancy, might draw on a number of existing methods or practices in other fields, including robust control (the study of control systems that can function in complex environments with multiple sources of noise or uncertainty)[11] and model checking (mathematical methods to explore all possible interactions within complex systems, such as computer chips),[12] among others. This is not a trivial endeavor but one that requires investment in basic research to bring multiple communities together and to

---

[10] Dario Amodei, Chris Olah, Jacob Steinhardt, Paul Christiano, John Shulman, and Dan Mané, "Concrete Problems in AI Safety," paper, ArXiv preprint, July 25, 2016.

[11] Kemin Zhou and John C. Doyle, *Essentials of Robust Control*, Upper Saddle River, N.J.: Prentice Hall, 1999.

[12] Edmund M. Clarke, Jr., Orna Grumberg, and Doron Peleg, *Model Checking*, MIT Press, 1999.

overcome difficulties traditional testing and evaluation methods will have in assessing AI systems. It would be remiss not to consider additional investments in basic research aiming to fundamentally change the design paradigm from one in which design and validation and verification are seen as discrete activities to one in which easy validation and verification are key considerations in the design process itself, perhaps even producing systems that are "correct by design," i.e., systems that need no further verification or validation.

New Test and Evaluation Techniques

An effective testing and evaluation system is essential to giving U.S. military personnel the confidence necessary to unleash the full potential of their AI systems. Unfortunately, the current DoD testing and evaluation system is not equipped to certify the reliability of autonomous systems effectively.[13] Machine-learning–based systems change their behavior over time in response to lessons learned, and current DoD testing and evaluation procedures are not designed to deal with such emergent behaviors. DoD test ranges are not equipped to represent the massively complex, open, unpredictable, and adversarial environments autonomous platforms will be operating in.[14] Current policies consider the performance of operators and systems separately, instead of evaluating their ability to achieve their objectives together. DoD verification and validation focus heavily on extensive reviews of the entire system in the last stages of its development, not on evaluating its component parts as they are developed. Finally, current testing and evaluation processes rely heavily on evaluations of previous platforms (i.e., the evaluation of the current main battle tank is closely tied to that of previous tanks), creating problems for novel autonomous systems with no predecessors.

Although some of these issues, such as test range improvement, will be very difficult to address and will require major reforms, there are some relatively straightforward steps that can be taken to improve DoD's testing and evaluation system's ability to build trust in autonomous systems. In line with current thinking on software development processes,[15] an important immediate fix would be to move most VVT&E activities for autonomous systems "to the left" in the development cycle, so that verification and validation work plays a greater role in defining

---

[13] Office of the Assistant Secretary of Defense for Research and Engineering, *Technology Investment Strategy: 2015–2018*, Washington, D.C.: Autonomy Community of Interest (COI), Test and Evaluation, Verification and Validation (TEVV) Working Group, May 2015, pp. 4–7. For a similar review of the challenges posed by the traits of AI systems, see Defense Science Board, *Task Force Report: The Role of Autonomy in DoD Systems*, Washington, D.C.: Office of the Under Secretary of Defense for Acquisition, Technology, and Logistics, July 2012.

[14] The cyberwar community is also struggling with the issue of designing test ranges that can evaluate its new weapon systems (both offensive and defensive). The community's experiences in designing cyberwar test ranges are producing valuable lessons that could benefit the military AI community. See Peter H. Christensen, "Cybersecurity T&E and the National Cyber Range: 'Top 10' Lessons Learned," briefing, 31st Annual National Test & Evaluation Conference, March 2–3, 2016.

[15] Donald Firesmith, "Four Types of Shift Left Testing," podcast, Software Engineering Institute website, September 2015.

and laying out early system requirements. Because autonomous control software is built on many layers of code and algorithms, verifying and validating the software's more-basic components early in the development process can certify its overall reliability more effectively and prevent costly fixes in later stages of development if problems are discovered in basic components.

While autonomous systems should not be judged by the standards of earlier manned platforms, each new software iteration can be evaluated based on its differences with its previous, already-validated version without the need for a lengthy review process of each update. Rapid prototyping can help build trust in system reliability and alleviate the problem of having no data from past autonomous systems to use as benchmarks for the new, groundbreaking systems under development. Wargames or simulations should be used to test new tactics or strategies, especially when playing against AI-enabled opponents. Wargames and simulations should also be used to test and verify the performance of decision aids, especially operational command algorithms or techniques for decisionmaking. Finally, the DoD test and evaluation process for AI should also begin to evaluate platforms and their operators as a single system to ensure that human-machine interaction can be optimized.[16]

Create Development, Test, and Evaluation Processes for New Operational Concepts that Employ AI Technologies

Wargaming and Operational Concepts

Historically, decisive military innovations have required comparable (although not necessarily superior) technology levels, organizations that can integrate new technology, and clear concepts of how technology will be used on the battlefield.[17] Because most of the fundamental technology behind AI is available to both Washington and Beijing and because both are developing similar new organizational structures in parallel, the United States must develop superior operational concepts to maintain a decisive advantage in AI applications.

One approach to developing such concepts will be through analytical wargaming.[18] In the past, such games have helped the U.S. military identify the new operational concepts and doctrines that enabled it to turn new technologies, such as the aircraft carrier and nuclear weapons, into decisive military advantages. A wargaming program to evaluate AI-enabled

---

[16] For a recent study of the challenges of human-machine teaming in military operations, see Mick Ryan, *Human-Machine Teaming for Future Ground Forces*, Washington, D.C.: Center for Strategic and Budgetary Assessments, 2018, especially pp. 17–30.

[17] For a good overview of the theory of military innovation, see Stephen Peter Rosen, *Winning the Next War: Innovation and the Modern Military*, Ithaca, N.Y.: Cornell University Press, 1991. For an excellent collection of essays on military innovation around the world in the interwar period, see Williamson Murray and Allan R. Millett, eds., *Military Innovation in the Interwar Period*, New York: Cambridge University Press, 1996.

[18] For a good primer on analytical wargaming methods and techniques, see Peter P. Perla, *The Art of Wargaming: A Guide for Professionals and Hobbyists*, Annapolis, Md.: Naval Institute Press, 1990.

operational concepts should start with parallel war games played by working-level members of the joint community and should be based on a possible conflict. In one of these games, the Blue force would have capabilities based on current programs of record; in another, it would have a variety of AI capabilities possible within the next few years, such as small swarming drones and autonomous F-16 wingmen for other USAF fighters. Using the results of these games, the Air Force professional military education institutions could consult with private-sector experts to build two or three operational concepts for using new AI-enabled capabilities. These could then be evaluated in a second set of war games covering possible conflicts to evaluate which of the operational concepts is most effective. The best concept(s) could then be distilled into a doctrinal white paper for the review and approval of the Air Staff and further evaluation in field experiments.

Integration into Multidomain Operations

The U.S. Army and Marine Corps developed the multidomain operations (MDO) concept to effectively meet new threats from adversaries that are able to confront the U.S. military in all six domains (air, land, sea, space, the electromagnetic spectrum, and cyberspace), able to launch long-distance precision strikes on U.S. forces, and able to operate in gray zones short of full-scale conflict.[19] This concept calls on U.S. forces to build new capabilities, including the ability to compete with adversaries in the gray zone and prepare for escalation of gray-zone conflicts into full-scale conflicts, and to calibrate force posture by ensuring that there are sufficient supplies in theater to rapidly flow forces into the region. MDO further postulates that the United States will need to build resilient formations able to operate when surrounded by enemy forces and facing a contested air environment and to launch coordinated operations in different domains, taking advantage of windows of superiority in any domain to affect other domains.

Some Artificial Intelligence–Enabled Air Force Tactical Concepts for Multidomain Operations

To respond effectively to the new threat environment, MDO posits four key ideas for U.S. joint forces: competition, calibration of force posture, employment of resilient formations, and converge capabilities. We believe that USAF forces could contribute heavily to the MDO vision through the use of four tactical concepts that are enabled by the new AI-driven autonomous systems that are coming online. Each tactical concept is aligned with one of the four tenets of the MDO vision.

The first concept, intelligent intelligence, surveillance, and reconnaissance (ISR) data processing, would support the competition tenet. This nonkinetic intelligence and surveillance concept would use AI-driven algorithms to sift through reams of data from overhead ISR assets

---

[19] The MDO concept is laid out in detail in U.S. Army Training and Doctrine Command, *Multi-Domain Battle: Evolution of Combined Arms for the 21st Century,* Vers. 1.0, October 2017.

(imagery and signals intelligence). It is likely that new and emerging AI early warning algorithms that are built on data from the major conflict outbreaks of the past will be able to pick up signs earlier than human analysts can.

The second tactical concept, AI-driven command and control, is designed to support the calibrating force posture component. This tactical concept would use AI-driven command-and-control and logistics systems to rapidly coordinate the movement of follow-on USAF combat air squadrons into a theater.

The third concept, autonomous weapons shield, would support the employment of resilient formations. This concept involves the use of USAF unmanned, autonomous loitering platforms to provide basic close air support.

The fourth tactical concept, AI optimization, is a command-and-control–oriented concept that would support the convergence tenet. This concept would use AI-driven dynamic mission-planning software to complete the current phase of the campaign.

Testing the New Concepts Through Field Exercises

Recent reports in the open defense press indicate that the U.S. Army has decided that the best way to test MDO ideas in field exercises is to eschew narrow proof-of-concept exercises, which are conducted with specially trained test units and, instead, incorporate experimental MDO tenets into regularly scheduled training exercises conducted by regular units to see whether those tenets are viable. While this approach might work for the Army today, we believe that the USAF should revert to the more-traditional proof-of-concept approach with special test units if it wishes to test new AI-driven tactical concepts that could be embedded into MDO sometime in the future.

The new tactical concepts we have proposed here push the envelope of current military science and depend on a high level of performance by AI systems and software that are still in the development phase. These concepts also depend on new types of tactics, techniques, and procedures that have not yet been used by Air Force personnel at any level. For field exercises to be useful in testing these ideas, it would be best for Air Force units that have been specially trained on potential new AI tactics, techniques, and procedures and systems to conduct specific, highly tailored proof-of-concept experiments outside normal training events.

4. Conclusions and Future Research

Conclusions

Our current assessment is that the United States currently has a modest lead over the PRC in AI technology development. This is largely because the United States has had a substantial advantage over China in the advanced semiconductor design and manufacturing sector because the U.S. sector is currently more capable and advanced than China's. A strong semiconductor industry is an essential foundation for good, solid AI research. However, the Chinese government is attempting to erode the U.S. edge through massive investment in the Chinese semiconductor industry.[1] Also, the Chinese semiconductor industry has the additional advantage of proximity to the enormous Chinese market.[2] This situation is further aggravated by the current lack of a substantial U.S. industrial policy.[3]

The United States and China are on more-equal terms when it comes to the dynamism of the two countries' tech-sector venture capitalists, but the United States may have the edge when it comes to a firmly established legal system and freedom of the press—together, these fundamental structural factors provide a stable foundation for AI development. The decoupling of the U.S. and Chinese tech sectors will provide a good test of how well the United States and China can compete separated. The PRC is certainly able to funnel considerable funds into AI research, but can AI in the PRC thrive in a vacuum, isolated from the US tech sector?

The PRC does have an advantage over the United States in the area of big data sets, which are essential to the development of AI applications. This is in part because the Chinese regime and the large Chinese tech companies (such as Alibaba) are able to harvest much more personal data from the Chinese populace than U.S. tech firms can harvest from the U.S. populace because of the lack of real privacy laws and protections in China. Also, the Chinese population is about four times larger than the U.S. population, so Chinese tech firms have an inherently larger latent

---

[1] For example,

> In the period since September 2014, numerous provinces and municipalities have established their own IC [integrated circuit] Funds, or received capital from the National IC Fund to establish other IC-related funds. Reports on the establishment of IC Funds in Hubei, Fujian, and Anhui provinces indicate the high degree of Chinese government involvement in establishing the funds in order to meet national strategic objectives. According to the SIA, provincial and municipal IC funds have raised a staggering sum—more than $80 billion. (Office of the U.S. Trade Representative, *Findings of the Investigation into China's Acts, Policies, and Practices Related to Technology Transfer, Intellectual Property, and Innovation Under Section 301 of the Trade Act of 1974*, Washington, D.C.: Executive Office of the President, March 22, 2018, pp. 93–94)

[2] Tekla S. Perry, "U.S. Semiconductor Industry Veterans Keep Wary Eyes on China," *IEEE Spectrum*, October 10, 2019.

[3] Perry, 2019.

database to draw from, even without taking into account the lax privacy protections in China. Overall, however, we believe that the Chinese advantage in data volume is not enough to overcome the U.S. edge in semiconductors. Thus, we judge that the United States currently has a modest lead over the PRC in AI.

It is important for DoD leadership to keep in mind that, ultimately, the long-term prospects for maintaining a lead over the Chinese military in AI-enabled systems, weapons, and operational concepts will, at least indirectly, depend on the ability of the United States to keep its edge over China in AI at the national level. Thus, USAF, as an institution, should do as much as it reasonably can to contribute to the overall national effort to maintain the country's position as the world leader in AI. For example, a promising option is for the USAF to financially support promising dual-use AI research projects in the private sector through the judicious awarding of Air Force contracts. Another option would be for the Air Force to work with DARPA to jointly sponsor and fund promising academic AI research that would have broad spinoff effects in the commercial sector. However, we conclude that, to maintain competitive advantage, the majority of Air Force resources should be devoted to the dimensions over which it has direct control: development and engineering to transition AI to the military, advances in VVT&E, and development of operational concepts.

Table 4.1 presents a framework for how we believe the USAF should allocate its near-term efforts in the area of AI development. It illustrates that, as we have argued in this report, the areas of basic research and technology commercialization call for a relatively low level of activity on the part of the Air Force because the global market for AI research is currently wide open and because there is little chance that the United States can gain an advantage over China in these parts of the AI development spectrum. We assess that a high-level effort is required in the area of transition to military applications. As part of this effort there should be a focus on improving the USAF's organic human capital for AI by working to recruit and retain more high-quality scientists and engineers with skills in the field. As we have shown in the body of this report, there are a number of ways to improve the S&T personnel pipeline into the USAF's research labs. Finally, we recommend that the USAF devote high levels of effort to the VVT&E and operational concept development phases of the spectrum. In these areas, USAF can gain a real operational advantage over the PLA by deploying more-reliable and user-friendly AI systems and by employing operational concepts that fully leverage the available technology by using system-of-systems approach that draws on U.S. strengths in other areas, such as advanced logistics management, autonomous small-unit operations, and flexible air basing infrastructures.

Table 4.1. Allocating USAF Effort Levels Across the Spectrum of AI Technology Development

	Fundamental Research	Advances in Commercial Industry	Transition to Military	VVT&E	Operational Concept Development
USAF activity level	Low	Low	High	High	High
Activities	Monitor global research activity. Support where possible.	Monitor global commercial activity. Support where possible.	Improve the human capital level of USAF scientists and engineers	Develop new ways of building validation techniques into early system design and requirements setting	Use extensive wargaming and field exercises to develop and refine innovative operational concepts, including new paradigms for using ISR

Using open-source materials alone, it is difficult, if not impossible, to arrive at a definitive statement about which country has the lead in AI and what the trends look like. Indeed, there may not be a single lead; it may be more useful to break AI into its constituents and talk about various parts of the AI ecosystem. Additionally, some of the data we might need are not publicly available, while others—such as assessments of culture and institutional focus—do not lend themselves to quantitative assessment. It is therefore challenging and of questionable merit to pursue an overall metric for "AI ecosystem lead." Overall, our data collection and analysis lead us to tentatively conclude that the United States has a narrow lead in a number of key areas of AI, while also noting that China has several advantages and a high degree of leadership focus on this issue. This assessment implies that the United States has little room for error and needs to focus attention and resources on ensuring that China does not open up a substantial lead over the United States in what appears likely to be a critical technology not only for the commercial economy that undergirds U.S. national power but also, specifically, for military applications in the broad defense space, most particularly including the aerospace domain.

Future Research

This report has concentrated on a preliminary comparative analysis of AI in China and the United States and what this means for USAF. We have merely scratched the surface, and much more research remains to be done to flesh out key dimensions, components, and factors that will affect the future of AI in China. The following topics may be particularly fruitful areas of inquiry; each can either serve as a stand-alone research project or become a component in a broader research effort:

- Map out the interactions and relationships among key military and civilian individuals in China's AI network. Learning more about key individuals, who they interact with, and how frequently can provide valuable insights into the trajectory of China's AI strategy.

- Map out the linkages and relationships among different military, political, academic, and commercial institutions in China's AI network, both inside and outside China's borders. Learning more about institutional relationships can offer significant insights into the trajectory of China's AI strategy.
- Follow the funding—how much, where does it come from, and where does it go? Following the money in China is not always possible and never easy, but it is surprising how much information can be gleaned from open sources. Monitoring the flow of funds is an important way to discern China's AI priorities and to assess how effectively AI funding is being spent.
- Focus on a single case study—of either a specific AI program or a specific AI entity of special interest. Zeroing in on a particular program or organization can provide considerable detail on what the implementation of the larger AI strategy means in practice.
- Concentrate on the PLA. Who are the key players, and what are the key entities? What AI research is being conducted by military research institutions, in terms of both theory and technology? How well does PLA doctrine incorporate AI? What is the process for applying AI to actual weapon systems and equipment? How are commanders and military units employing AI?

References

Alderman, Daniel, and Jonathan Ray, "Artificial Intelligence, Emerging Technologies, and China-US Strategic Competition," in Tai Ming Cheung and Thomas G. Mahnken, eds., *The Gathering Pacific Storm: Emerging US-China Strategic Competition in Defense Technological and Industrial Development*, Amherst, N.Y.: Cambria Press, 2018, pp. 179–210.

Amodei, Dario, Chris Olah, Jacob Steinhardt, Paul Christiano, John Shulman, and Dan Mané, "Concrete Problems in AI Safety," paper, ArXiv preprint, July 25, 2016. As of April 13, 2020:
https://arxiv.org/abs/1606.06565v1

Bell, Daniel A., *China's New Confucianism: Politics and Everyday Life in a Changing Society*, Princeton, N.J.: Princeton University Press, 2008.

Blinde, Loren, "Army to Host 3rd Annual DoD AI Industry Day," Intelligence Community News website, October 16, 2019. As of April 10, 2020:
https://intelligencecommunitynews.com/army-to-host-3rd-annual-dod-ai-industry-day/

CB Insights, "Top AI Trends to Watch in 2018," New York, 2018.

Chase, Michael S., Jeffrey Engstrom, Tai Ming Cheung, Kristen A. Gunness, Scott Warren Harold, Susan Puska, and Samuel K. Berkowitz, *China's Incomplete Military Transformation: Assessing the Weaknesses of People's Liberation Army (PLA)*, Santa Monica, Calif.: RAND Corporation, RR-893-USCC, 2015. As of April 10, 2020:
https://www.rand.org/pubs/research_reports/RR893.html

Cheung, Tai Ming, *Fortifying China: The Struggle to Build a Modern Defense Economy*, Ithaca, N.Y.: Cornell University Press, 2009.

———, "An Uncertain Transition: Regulatory Reform and Industrial Innovation in China's Defense Research, Development and Acquisition System," in Tai Ming Cheung, ed., *Forging China's Military Might: A New Framework for Assessing Innovation*, Baltimore, Md.: Johns Hopkins University Press, 2014a.

———, ed., *Forging China's Military Might: A New Framework for Assessing Innovation*, Baltimore, Md.: Johns Hopkins University Press, 2014b.

Cheung, Tai Ming, Thomas G. Mahnken, and Andrew L. Ross, "Frameworks for Analyzing Chinese Defense and Military Innovation," in Tai Ming Cheung, *Forging China's Military Might: A New Framework for Assessing Innovation*, Baltimore, Md.: Johns Hopkins University Press, 2014.

Chow, Irene Hau-Siu, "The Relationship Between Entrepreneurial Orientation and Firm Performance in China," *SAM Advanced Management Journal,* Vol. 71, No. 3, Summer 2006, pp. 16–19.

"The Chips Are Down: The Semiconductor Industry and the Power of Globalisation," *The Economist,* December 1, 2018. As of April 10, 2020:
https://www.economist.com/briefing/2018/12/01/the-semiconductor-industry-and-the-power-of-globalisation

Christensen, Peter H., "Cybersecurity T&E and the National Cyber Range: 'Top 10' Lessons Learned," briefing, 31st Annual National Test & Evaluation Conference, March 2–3, 2016.

Clarke, Edmund M., Jr., Orna Grumberg, and Doron Peleg, *Model Checking*, MIT Press, 1999.

Crevier, Daniel, *AI: The Tumultuous History of the Search for Artificial Intelligence*, Basic Books, 1993.

DARPA—*See* Defense Advanced Research Projects Agency.

Decker, Gilbert, Robert A. Beaudet, Siddhartha Dalal, Jay Davis, William H. Forster, George T. Singley III, David E. Mosher, Caroline Reilly, Phil Kehres, Gary Cecchine, and Nicholas C. Maynard, *Improving Army Basic Research: Report of an Expert Panel on the Future of Army Laboratories*, Santa Monica, Calif.: RAND Corporation, MG-1176-A, 2012. As of April 10, 2020:
https://www.rand.org/pubs/monographs/MG1176.html

Defense Advanced Research Projects Agency, "DARPA Announces $2 Billion Campaign to Develop Next Wave of AI Technologies," press release, September 7, 2018. As of April 10, 2020:
https://www.darpa.mil/news-events/2018-09-07

———, "DARPA Electronics Resurgence Initiative," webpage, December 19, 2019. As of December 2019:
https://www.darpa.mil/work-with-us/electronics-resurgence-initiative

Defense Science Board, *Task Force Report: The Role of Autonomy in DoD Systems*, Washington, D.C.: Office of the Under Secretary of Defense for Acquisition, Technology, and Logistics, July 2012. As of April 13, 2020:
https://fas.org/irp/agency/dod/dsb/autonomy.pdf

Dickson, Bruce J., *Wealth into Power: The Communist Party's Embrace of China's Private Sector*, New York: Cambridge University Press, 2008.

Ding, Jeffrey, *Deciphering China's AI Dream: The Context, Components, Capabilities, and Consequences of China's Strategy to Lead the World in AI*, Oxford, U.K.: Future of

Humanity Institute, University of Oxford, March 2018. As of April 10, 2020:
https://www.fhi.ox.ac.uk/wp-content/uploads/Deciphering_Chinas_AI-Dream.pdf

Executive Order 13859, *Maintaining American Leadership in Artificial Intelligence*, February
11, 2019. As of April 16, 2020:
https://www.federalregister.gov/documents/2019/02/14/2019-02544/maintaining-american-
leadership-in-artificial-intelligence

Felten, Ed, "Preparing for the Future of Artificial Intelligence," White House Office of Science
and Technology Policy blog, May 3, 2016. As of April 10, 2020:
https://obamawhitehouse.archives.gov/blog/2016/05/03/preparing-future-artificial-
intelligence

Firesmith, Donald, "Four Types of Shift Left Testing," podcast, Software Engineering Institute
website, September 2015. As of April 13, 2020:
https://resources.sei.cmu.edu/library/asset-view.cfm?assetid=447143

Foner, Eric, *The Story of American Freedom*, New York: Norton, 1999.

Fukuyama, Francis, *Trust: The Social Virtues and the Creation of Prosperity*, New York: Free
Press, 1995.

Geert Hofstede website, undated. As of April 13, 2020:
https://geerthofstede.com/

Geertz, Clifford, *The Interpretation of Cultures: Selected Essays*, New York: Basic Books, 1973.

Hoadley, Daniel S., and Nathan J. Lucas, *Artificial Intelligence and National Security*,
Washington, D.C.: Congressional Research Service, April 26, 2018.

Hofstede, Geert, *Culture's Consequences: Comparing Values, Behaviors, Institutions, and
Organizations Across Nations*, 2nd ed., Thousand Oaks, Calif.: Sage Publications, 2001.

Hofstede, Geert, and Gert Jan Hofstede, *Cultures and Organizations: Software of the Mind*, 2nd
ed., New York: McGraw-Hill, 2005.

James, Geoffrey, *Business Wisdom of the Electronic Elite*, New York: Random House, 1996.

———, "Bill Gates Told Me This 25 Years Ago and It's Still Freakin' Brilliant," *Inc.*,
September 17, 2019. As of April 13, 2020:
https://www.inc.com/geoffrey-james/bill-gates-told-me-this-25-years-ago-its-still-freakin-
brilliant.html

Ji, You, *China's Military Transformation*, Cambridge, Mass.: Polity Press, 2016.

Jones, Michael L., "Hofstede—Culturally Questionable?" paper presented at the 2007 Oxford
Business and Economics Conference, Oxford, UK, June 24–26, 2007. As of April 13, 2020:

https://ro.uow.edu.au/cgi/viewcontent.cgi?referer=https://scholar.google.com/&httpsredir=1&article=1389&context=commpapers

Jordan, Michael, "Artificial Intelligence—The Revolution Hasn't Happened Yet," Medium website, April 19, 2018. As of April 13, 2020:
https://medium.com/@mijordan3/artificial-intelligence-the-revolution-hasnt-happened-yet-5e1d5812e1e7

Joske, Alex, *Picking Flowers, Making Honey: The Chinese Military's Collaboration with Foreign Universities*, Canberra: International Cyber Policy Center, Australian Strategic Policy Institute, 2018. As of April 14, 2020:
https://www.aspi.org.au/report/picking-flowers-making-honey

Kania, Elsa B., "Chinese Military Innovation in Artificial Intelligence," testimony before the U.S.-China Economic and Security Review Commission Hearing on Trade, Technology, and Military-Civil Fusion, June 7, 2019. As of April 13, 2020:
https://www.uscc.gov/sites/default/files/June%207%20Hearing_Panel%201_Elsa%20Kania_Chinese%20Military%20Innovation%20in%20Artificial%20Intelligence_0.pdf

Khan, Yusuf, "Chinese Investment into the US Has Plunged 90% Since Trump Took Office—and Poorer States May Get Hit the Hardest," Business Insider website, July 22, 2019. As of April 13, 2020:
https://markets.businessinsider.com/news/stocks/china-investment-us-drying-up-poor-states-michigan-lose-out-2019-7-1028371155

Lee, Kai-Fu, *AI Superpowers: China, Silicon Valley and the New World Order*, Boston: Houghton Mifflin Harcourt, 2018.

Levenson, Joseph R., *Confucian China and Its Modern Fate: A Trilogy*, in three volumes, Berkeley, Calif.: University of California Press, 1958–1965.

Lieberthal, Kenneth, *Governing China: From Revolution Through Reform,* 2nd ed. New York: W.W. Norton, 2004.

Ling, Weipeng, Lei Wang, and Shuting Chen, "Abusive Supervision and Employee Well-Being: The Moderating Effect of Power Distance Orientation," *Applied Psychology,* Vol. 62, No. 2, 2013, pp. 308–329. As of January 21, 2020:
https://onlinelibrary.wiley.com/doi/pdf/10.1111/j.1464-0597.2012.00520.x

Marcus, Gary, "Deep Learning: A Critical Appraisal," paper, undated. As of April 13, 2020:
https://arxiv.org/ftp/arxiv/papers/1801/1801.00631.pdf

Mattis, James, *Summary of the 2018 National Defense Strategy of the United States of America: Sharpening the American Military's Competitive Edge*, Washington, D.C.: U.S. Department of Defense, 2018.

McNeill, William H., *The Pursuit of Power*, Chicago: University of Chicago Press, 1982.

Metz, Cade, "As China Marches Forward on A.I., the White House Is Silent," *New York Times,* February 12, 2018. As of April 10, 2020:
https://www.nytimes.com/2018/02/12/technology/china-trump-artificial-intelligence.html

———, "Trump Signs Executive Order Promoting Artificial Intelligence," *New York Times,* February 11, 2019. As of April 10, 2020:
https://www.nytimes.com/2019/02/11/business/ai-artificial-intelligence-trump.html

"Ministry of Science and Technology Announces its First 4 National New Generation A.I. Innovation Platforms, As Well As Its 27 Member Strategic Consultative Committee [科技部首批4家国家新一代人工智能开放创新平台，27位战略咨询委员会名单]," Sohu.com website, November 19, 2017. As of April 10, 2020:
https://www.sohu.com/a/205421972_784996

Mistreanu, Simina, "Beyond 'Decoupling': How China Will Reshape Global Trade in 2020," *Forbes*, December 3, 2019. As of April 13, 2020:
https://www.forbes.com/sites/siminamistreanu/2019/12/03/beyond-decoupling-how-china-will-reshape-global-trade-in-2020/#32ceedc265b7

Murray, Williamson, and Allan R. Millett, eds., *Military Innovation in the Interwar Period*, New York: Cambridge University Press, 1996.

Nathan, Andrew J., and Andrew Scobell, *China's Search for Security*, New York: Columbia University Press, 2012.

National Science and Technology Council, *The National Artificial Intelligence Research and Development Strategic Plan*, Washington, D.C.: Executive Office of the President, October 2016. As of April 16, 2020:
https://www.nitrd.gov/pubs/national_ai_rd_strategic_plan.pdf

———, *The National Artificial Intelligence Research and Development Strategic Plan*, Washington, D.C.: Executive Office of the President, June 2019. As of April 13, 2020:
https://www.nitrd.gov/pubs/National-AI-RD-Strategy-2019.pdf

National Security Commission on Artificial Intelligence, "Interim Report," November 2019. As of April 16, 2020:
https://www.epic.org/foia/epic-v-ai-commission/AI-Commission-Interim-Report-Nov-2019.pdf

Nicas, Jack, and Katie Benner, "F.B.I. Asks Apple to Help Unlock Two iPhones," *New York Times,* January 7, 2020. As of April 13, 2020:
https://www.nytimes.com/2020/01/07/technology/apple-fbi-iphone-encryption.html

Norris, William J., *Chinese Economic Statecraft: Commercial Actors, Grand Strategy, and State Control*, Ithaca, N.Y.: Cornell University Press, 2016.

Office of the Assistant Secretary of Defense for Research and Engineering, *Technology Investment Strategy: 2015–2018*, Washington, D.C.: Autonomy Community of Interest (COI), Test and Evaluation, Verification and Validation (TEVV) Working Group, May 2015. As of April 13, 2020:
https://defenseinnovationmarketplace.dtic.mil/wp-content/uploads/2018/02/OSD_ATEVV_STRAT_DIST_A_SIGNED.pdf

Office of the U.S. Trade Representative, *Findings of the Investigation into China's Acts, Policies, and Practices Related to Technology Transfer, Intellectual Property, and Innovation Under Section 301 of the Trade Act of 1974*, Washington, D.C.: Executive Office of the President, March 22, 2018. As of April 10, 2020:
https://ustr.gov/sites/default/files/Section%20301%20FINAL.PDF

Paine, Jocelyn, "W is for Winter," *AI Expert Newsletter*, January 2005. As of January 20, 2020. As of April 13, 2020:
https://web.archive.org/web/20131109201636/http://www.ainewsletter.com/newsletters/aix_0501.htm#w

Perla, Peter P., *The Art of Wargaming: A Guide for Professionals and Hobbyists*, Annapolis, Md.: Naval Institute Press, 1990.

Perry, Elizabeth J., "From Mass Campaigns to Managed Campaigns: 'Constructing a New Socialist Countryside,'" in Sebastian Heilmann and Elizabeth J. Perry, eds., *Mao's Invisible Hand: The Political Foundations of Adaptive Governance in China*, Cambridge, Mass: Harvard University Asia Center, 2011, pp. 30–62.

Perry, Tekla S., "U.S. Semiconductor Industry Veterans Keep Wary Eyes on China," *IEEE Spectrum*, October 10, 2019. As of April 10, 2020:
https://spectrum.ieee.org/view-from-the-valley/semiconductors/devices/semiconductor-industry-veterans-keep-wary-eyes-on-china

Public Law 115-232, John S. McCain National Defense Authorization Act for Fiscal Year 2019, August 13, 2018. As of May 22, 2020:
https://www.govinfo.gov/app/details/PLAW-115publ232

Putnam, Robert D., *Our Kids: The American Dream in Crisis*, New York: Simon and Schuster, 2015.

Pye, Lucian W., *Asian Power and Politics: The Cultural Dimensions of Authority*, Cambridge, Mass.: Belknap Press, 1985.

Roland, Alex, and Philip Shiman, *Strategic Computing: DARPA and the Quest for Machine Intelligence, 1983–1993*, MIT Press, 2002.

Rosen, Stephen Peter, *Winning the Next War: Innovation and the Modern Military*, Ithaca, N.Y.: Cornell University Press, 1991.

Rowan, Henry S., Marguerite Gong Hancock, and William F. Miller, eds., *Greater China's Quest for Innovation*, Stanford, Calif.: Walter H. Shorenstein Asia-Pacific Research Center, 2008.

Ryan, Mick, *Human-Machine Teaming for Future Ground Forces*, Washington, D.C.: Center for Strategic and Budgetary Assessments, 2018.

Schein, Edgar H., "Coming to a New Awareness of Organizational Culture," *Sloan Management Review*, Vol. 25, No. 2, January 15, 1984, pp. 3–16.

Schwartz, Benjamin I., *The World of Thought in Ancient China*, Cambridge, Mass.: Belknap Press of Harvard University, 1985.

Scobell, Andrew, *China's Use of Military Force: Beyond the Great Wall and the Long March*, New York: Cambridge University Press, 2003.

———, "China's Real Strategic Culture: A Great Wall of the Imagination," *Contemporary Security Policy,* Vol. 35, No. 2, August 2014, pp. 215–217.

Scobell, Andrew, Edmund J. Burke, Cortez A. Cooper III, Sale Lilly, Chad J. R. Ohlandt, Eric Warner, and J. D. Williams, *China's Grand Strategy: Trends, Trajectories, Long-Term Competition*, Santa Monica, Calif.: RAND Corporation, RR-2798-A, forthcoming.

Scobell, Andrew, and John M. Sanford, *North Korea's Military Threat: Pyongyang's Conventional Forces, Weapons of Mass Destruction, and Ballistic Missiles*, Carlisle Barracks, Pa.: U.S. Army War College Strategic Studies Institute, 2007.

Sedmak, Aileen, Office of the DASD (Systems Engineering), "Understanding the DoD's Engineering Workforce," briefing delivered at NDIA Systems Engineering Conference, October 29, 2015.

Shead, Sam, "DARPA Plans to Spend $2 Billion Developing New AI Technologies," *Forbes*, September 7, 2018. As of April 10, 2020: https://www.forbes.com/sites/samshead/2018/09/07/darpa-plans-to-spend-2-billion-developing-new-ai-technologies/#489f8ae73ae1

Simon, Denis Fred, and Cong Cao, *China's Emerging Technological Edge: Assessing the Role of High-End Talent*, New York: Cambridge University Press, 2009.

Smith, Samantha, "Most Think the 'American Dream' Is Within Reach for Them," Pew Research Center website, October 31, 2017. As of April 13, 2020:

https://www.pewresearch.org/fact-tank/2017/10/31/most-think-the-american-dream-is-within-reach-for-them/

Spencer-Oatey, Helen, "Unequal Relationships in High and Low Power Distance Societies: A Comparative Study of Tutor-Student Role Relations in Britain and China," *Journal of Cross-Cultural Psychology,* Vol. 28, No. 3, May 1997, pp. 284–302. As of April 13, 2020: https://journals.sagepub.com/doi/pdf/10.1177/0022022197283005

State Council of the People's Republic of China, *A New Generation Artificial Intelligence Development Plan,* trans. Graham Webster, Rogier Creemers, Paul Triolo, and Elsa Kania, July 20, 2017. As of April 13, 2020: https://www.newamerica.org/cybersecurity-initiative/digichina/blog/full-translation-chinas-new-generation-artificial-intelligence-development-plan-2017/

———, "State Council on the Adjustments to the National Science and Technology System Reform and Innovation System Construction Leading Small Group [国务院办公厅关于调整国家科技体制改革 和创新体系建设领导小组]," Guobanfa (2018), No. 86, September 7, 2018. As of April 10, 2020: http://www.gov.cn/zhengce/content/2018-09/07/content_5319966.htm

Tarraf, Danielle C., William Shelton, Edward Parker, Brien Alkire, Diana Gehlhaus Carew, Justin Grana, Alexis Levedahl, Jasmin Léveillé, Jared Mondschein, James Ryseff, Ali Wyne, Dan Elinoff, Edward Geist, Benjamin N. Harris, Eric Hui, Cedric Kenney, Sydne Newberry, Chandler Sachs, Peter Schirmer, Danielle Schlang, Victoria Smith, Abbie Tingstad, Padmaja Vedula, and Kristin Warren, *The Department of Defense Posture for Artificial Intelligence: Assessment and Recommendations*, Santa Monica, Calif.: RAND Corporation, RR-4229-OSD, 2019. As of April 10, 2020: https://www.rand.org/pubs/research_reports/RR4229.html

U.S. Army Training and Doctrine Command, *Multi-Domain Battle: Evolution of Combined Arms for the 21st Century,* Vers. 1.0, October 2017.

Wakabayashi, Daisuke, and Scott Shane, "Google Will Not Renew Pentagon Contract That Upset Employees," *New York Times,* June 1, 2018. As of April 13, 2020: https://www.nytimes.com/2018/06/01/technology/google-pentagon-project-maven.html

Wang, Zheng, *Never Forget National Humiliation: Historical Memory in Chinese Politics and Foreign Relations*, New York: Columbia University Press, 2014.

Waters, Richard, "Why We Are in Danger of Overestimating AI," *Financial Times*, February 5, 2018.

The White House, *National Security Strategy of the United States of America*, Washington, D.C., December 2017. As of April 14, 2020:
https://www.whitehouse.gov/wp-content/uploads/2017/12/NSS-Final-12-18-2017-0905.pdf

———, "Artificial Intelligence for the American People," fact sheet, May 10, 2018. As of April 10, 2020:
https://www.whitehouse.gov/briefings-statements/artificial-intelligence-american-people/.

———, "Artificial Intelligence for the American People," website, February 19, 2019. As of April 10, 2020:
https://www.whitehouse.gov/ai/

Wilson, James Q., *Bureaucracy: What Government Agencies Do and Why They Do It*, New York: Basic Books, 1989.

Wuthnow, Joel, and Phillip C. Saunders, *Chinese Military Reforms in the Age of Xi Jinping: Drivers, Challenges, and Implications*, Washington, D.C.: National Defense University Press, 2017.

Zhou, Kemin, and John C. Doyle, *Essentials of Robust Control*, Upper Saddle River, N.J.: Prentice Hall, 1999.

Zimmerman, S. Rebecca, Kimberly Jackson, Natasha Lander, Colin Roberts, Dan Madden, and Rebeca Orrie, *Movement and Maneuver: Culture and the Competition for Influence Among the U.S. Military Services*, Santa Monica, Calif.: RAND Corporation, RR-2270-OSD, 2019. As of April 10, 2020:
https://www.rand.org/pubs/research_reports/RR2270.html